THE
ESSENTIAL
Jack Russell Terrier

Featuring Photographs by
RENÉE STOCKDALE

Howell Book House®
An Imprint of
WILEY

Howell Book House

Howell Book House

Published by Wiley Publishing, Inc. All rights reserved
Published simultaneously in Canada

For general information about our other products and services, please contact our Customer Care Department within the United States at (800) 762-2974, outside the United States at (317) 572-3993 or fax (317) 572-4002.

Wiley also publishes its books in a variety of electronic formats. Some content that appears in print may not be available in electronic books. For more information about Wiley products, visit our web site at www.wiley.com.

The Essential Jack Russell Terrier is a revised edition of *The Jack Russell Terrier: An Owner's Guide to a Happy Healthy Pet,* first published in 1996.

Library of Congress Cataloging-in-Publication Data
The essential Jack Russell Terrier / featuring photographs by Renée Stockdale.
     p. cm.
    ISBN 0-87605-344-4
    1. Jack Russell terrier.   I. Howell Book House
SF429.J27E77 1998   98-3414
636.755—dc21   CIP
Manufactured in the United States of America
10 9 8

Series Directors: Dominique DeVito, Don Stevens
Series Assistant Director: Jennifer Liberts, Amanda Pisani
Editorial Assistant: Michele Matrisciani
Photography Editor: Sarah Storey
Book Design: Paul Costello
Photography:
  Front cover photo by Close Encounters of the Furry Kind/J. Harrison
  Courtesy of Diana Robinson: 77, 80, 81
  All other photos by Renée Stockdale.
  Many Jack Russell Terriers in interior photos courtesy of Rustic Pines Farm; Marc, Debra, Eli and CalliMae Malec and Emily Jean Edington.
Production Team: Stephanie Mohler, Jenaffer Brandt, Linda Quigley

CHAPTER ONE

Getting to Know Your Jack Russell Terrier

Before you bring a Jack Russell Terrier into your home, please consider carefully whether you can provide for all of the needs of this small-in-size, big-in-attitude dog. It is a mistake to think that being small makes a Jack Russell easy to keep. The JRT is a solid bundle of energy in a deceptively small package, an intelligent, demanding, always active hunting dog.

There are many pleasures in owning a Jack Russell. If you decide that you really do want to share your life with such a bright companion, you will find that you have embarked on a wonderful adventure in friendship with one of the most remarkable, energetic canine personalities.

A WORKING DOG

The Jack Russell Terrier, whose ancestors worked for a living hunting below ground, remains much the same animal he was nearly 200 years ago. One of the most intelligent dogs on (or in) the earth, with an activity level locked in the "on" position, Jack Russells are indisputably active and assertive. After a nap, they are ready for seemingly endless play or work.

Jack Russells Need Supervision

Jack Russells respond quickly and forcefully to their hunting instincts.

The most obedient, well-trained Jack Russell, out by himself or walking unleashed at your side, is likely to bolt at the sight of a squirrel or other animal on the other side of the road. A car or truck coming along at just the wrong moment can bring a sad end to your wonderful companion. Vehicular accidents are the most common cause of death to Jack Russells—and are, for the most part, avoidable by keeping your dog on leash.

Containing a Jack Russell can be difficult. They are bred to dig and can quickly escape under a sloppily built fenced area, particularly if the fence has not been buried a few inches into the ground. These dogs can jump more than 4 feet from a standstill and can climb, almost human-style, over a 10-foot or

Jack Russell Terriers were bred to be working dogs and are therefore as comfortable, if not more so, on the farm as they are inside the house.

2

higher fence. They certainly will not tolerate being tied up by a rope or chain—unthinkable for any dog, but especially for a Jack Russell. Kennel runs are excellent if they are long enough for the dog to move about freely and provide shade and shelter. They also should have a secure top to discourage climbing.

The very same Jack Russell that lovingly curls up in your lap and shares your bed will happily dash out the door, leaving you in the lurch as he runs off to go to work below ground. How frightening it is when your JRT disappears. It happens quite often. These dogs are primarily ruled by their instincts, and their safety must never be taken for granted.

A JRT is always sure of himself and can be quite single-minded about whatever he is focused on. He can be stubborn and persist in his activity to the point of exhaustion.

JACK RUSSELLS ARE LOVING

Although JRTs can be naughty, willful and wayward, they are quite devoted to, and want to be with, their favorite people. In fact,

Among the Jack Russell Terrier's many special traits is the ability to jump as high as 4 feet!

3

they can be quite possessive of those they love, wanting to guard them from children and even other pets.

Unlike many other types of dogs, Jack Russells enjoy direct eye contact. They will stare affectionately into the eyes of those they love, seemingly able to follow conversations. They enjoy hours of activity and play, knowing just how to entice you into their games, and, of course, desire close physical contact with their loved ones. They will happily cuddle up to their owners under the covers, or at least sleep near enough so they know when their people stir

A Dog's Senses

Sight: Dogs can detect movement at a greater distance than we can, but they can't see as well up close. They can also see better in less light, but can't distinguish many colors.

Sound: Dogs can hear about four times better than we can, and they can hear high-pitched sounds especially well. Their ancestors, the wolves, howled to let other wolves know where they were; our dogs do the same, but they have a wider range of vocalizations, including barks, whimpers, moans and whines.

Smell: A dog's nose is his greatest sensory organ. His sense of smell is so great he can follow a trail that's weeks old, detect odors diluted to one-millionth the concentration we'd need to notice them, even sniff out a person under water!

Taste: Dogs have fewer taste buds than we do, so they're likelier to try anything—and usually do, which is why it's especially important for their owners to monitor their food intake. Dogs are omnivores, which means they eat meat as well as vegetable matter, like grasses and weeds.

Touch: Dogs are social animals and love to be petted, groomed and played with. Jack Russells have a quiet side too, and are often happiest curled up next to the people they love.

and are sure not to miss anything. As a whole, JRTs remain almost puppylike through adulthood. They are willing, and happy, to work and play and be mischievous well into their senior years.

Jack Russells and Children

Jack Russells do not always fare well with children—and some children do not fare well with Jack Russells. These dogs will not tolerate rough treatment. If they are abused by a child, they may be inclined to discipline that child probably quite fairly, for the offense committed. They will not put up with having their ears pulled, being stepped on or hurt in any way. JRTs play very hard with each other, often causing concern in those watching their practice pounces and high-pitched, mouthy battles. Children must never engage in play with Jack Russells that in any way duplicates the terriers' practice-hunting play. Even normal play within terrier circles can be serious in nature: They exert their will on each other as practice for exerting their wills on formidable quarry. Jack Russells are not suitable

Jack Russells have an instinct to unearth quarry, of whatever kind, and nothing in your house is safe from the chase.

for small or undisciplined children and it is suggested that their time together be supervised at all times.

TALKATIVE

JRTs are not "yappy," but can be very vocal when someone comes to the door. Some will bark when left alone for a prolonged period of time by busy families who must be away from home.

VERSATILE AND ADAPTABLE

JRTs, with their good temperaments and love for people, can be fine companions and therapy dogs. They are intelligent, possess a wonderful sense of fun and can be loving, amusing and entertaining. They are well suited to assisting the deaf since they are attuned to such noises as buzzers and bells.

And they are adaptable. When displaced, needing a new home, they

CHARACTERISTICS OF THE JACK RUSSELL TERRIER

Extremely energetic

Independent

Needs supervision with small children

Strong hunting instincts

Intelligent

Willful

Extremely cute

settle in quickly to any new situation where they are loved and their needs are met. They have a never-look-back attitude if their present is full of affection and mental and physical activity.

RAISING YOUR JACK RUSSELL

With Another Pet

Although a JRT can be raised with a cat, there are many reported stories

Since Jack Russells are so energetic and willful, limit play between your new JRT and your children to those times when you are able to supervise.

of these friendships going wrong later when the two animals are left unattended. Jack Russells have been bred to have the courage to stand up to a fox, and if a fox is not available, a cat may do. It is just not a good idea to keep JRTs with cats, birds or pet rodents of any kind.

With Visitors

After thoroughly screening a visitor, some Russells will seem to smile and throw themselves at the person's feet waiting to be petted, but they can also show a fierce side when protecting their people and territory. A Jack Russell must never be allowed to believe he has a dominant position in "his family," his "pack." His owners must be consistent in showing strong leadership. JRTs need and respect the firm, fair administration of authority.

It is essential that a puppy be well socialized early to ensure that he grows into a stable, happy, well-adjusted dog. The breed standard describes shyness (not to be confused with sensitivity) and overaggression as serious faults. Aggressive behavior toward people or other dogs should never be tolerated, and

corrective training and strong guidance are required to eliminate this trait.

TRAINING YOUR JACK RUSSELL

Training Jack Russell Terriers can sometimes be a challenge. They will be brilliantly responsive, perfectly performing a task, and then start to yawn in total disinterest. They can be stubborn to the point of distraction. They do respond well to the tried and true methods of praise, reward, consistency—and good timing. If the training is too much of a boring drill, repeated over and

However cute the combination might seem, keeping a JRT in the house with other small pets, like cats, is not necessarily safe.

7

over for too long a time, results will be disappointing. The dog must perceive a purpose in the training and must enjoy himself in the process. If the activity is kept stimulating, many JRTs excel at and really enjoy obedience and agility competition.

Their independent natures will make training your Jack Russell a challenge sometimes, but beginning at a young age will make the process easier.

FUN AND GAMES

The Jack Russell Terrier has been admitted to the Miscellaneous Class of the American Kennel Club (AKC) and may compete in obedience trials sponsored by the AKC. Moreover, the Jack Russell Terrier Club of America hosts trials across the United States that include many different activities particularly suited to Jack Russells.

Jack Russells enjoy activities such as obedience, agility, fly ball and racing. Obedience, agility and fly ball classes are offered in many areas, and competition in these events, along with racing and go-to-ground, is offered at Jack Russell Terrier Trials throughout the country.

Sanctioned trials offer competition in conformation, obedience and agility classes and certificates for achievement.

CHAPTER TWO

Homecoming

With preparation and planning, the arrival in your home of your puppy or adult dog will be a happy event. Jack Russells adjust very quickly to new situations and adapt themselves nicely to a new home.

Visit your new puppy a few times before bringing her home. It is also good to meet the dam (mother) and the sire (father) to give you a better understanding of the personality and characteristics your dog may have. A good disposition is a must.

For the first few days, try to keep visitors and activities to a minimum. Give your new family member a bit of time to become acclimated to her people and her surroundings.

EQUIPMENT

Rather than forget something, or have to settle for what you don't really like, take your time shopping and have your new puppy's supplies ready.

Crate

You will need a crate, of course, with a pad and bedding inside. You might

A crate is an important item to have among your pet supplies.

10

also want to get another small bed for use outside of the crate. Puppies need a lot of sleep, and snuggling into a comfy soft bed will give them the support and feeling of security they need to sleep well.

Food and Water Bowls

Sturdy crock bowls for food and water are very good for terriers. They are difficult to tip over and difficult for your puppy to pick up and carry off to who-knows-where.

Leash and Collar

You will need a leash and a collar or collars that fit properly at all stages of growth. Rolled leather collars work very well and are comfortable. Be certain to adjust the collar so

that it fits securely but not tightly, and check it on a regular basis, particularly as your puppy grows. (The collar should be snug enough that it will not slip over the head, but loose enough to allow you to comfortably insert two or three fingers between the collar and the neck.)

A nylon leash may be best for puppies, who find great joy in chewing leather leashes. Make sure the clip is a sturdy one that will not release accidentally. A leather leash is recommended for JRTs past the teething stage.

PUPPY-PROOFING YOUR HOME

With a new terrier in your home, you will need to do some thorough puppy-proofing. Potted plants within reach of your JRT, for example, provide an ideal place to practice a skill that comes naturally to her: digging. Worse than the inconvenience of an upended plant, though, is the fact that many common houseplants and garden plants can be deadly to your dog if ingested.

Of course, medicines also must be kept out of reach of your terrier. (For a JRT, out-of-reach places do not include tables or countertops.)

And don't forget to put away the chocolates—all of it. Unfortunately, a dog can be poisoned after eating what would seem to us to be just a little bit of chocolate.

Remember that a very small amount of toxin can have a big impact on a small dog. Household chemicals and cleaning supplies should be secured out of reach of your dog, and don't overlook all the things stored in the garage or spilled on the garage floor. Antifreeze has a pleasant taste to dogs and lapping up just a little bit can prove fatal.

Limiting the area in which your pup is allowed to roam will make housetraining considerably easier. Gates provide good barriers between rooms and letting your dog romp in an exercise pen will make him happy and keep him safe. Finally, a crate is an invaluable tool for the protection and well-being of your dog.

Crate-Training

Jack Russells love their crates and use them as dens. When the door is left open and there is a comfortable bed inside, the dog will seek it by choice for privacy and rest. Either a wire crate or an airline carrier is suitable, as long as it is large enough for a grown terrier to stand up in and turn around comfortably. The bed or pad inside should be one that is not easily torn. An added baby blanket will let a puppy snuggle in

HOUSEHOLD DANGERS

Curious puppies and inquisitive dogs get into trouble not because they are bad, but simply because they want to investigate the world around them. It's our job to protect our dogs from harmful substances, like the following:

In the House

cleaners, especially pine oil

perfumes, colognes, aftershaves

medications, vitamins

office and craft supplies

electric cords

chicken or turkey bones

chocolate

onions

some house and garden plants, like ivy,
    oleander and poinsettia

In the Garage

antifreeze

garden supplies, like snail and slug bait, pesti-
    cides, fertilizers and mouse and rat poisons

11

Puppies, especially Jack Russell Terrier puppies, are curious by nature, so puppy-proofing your home is an important step toward keeping them out of trouble.

and help provide warmth and protection from drafts. Keeping some stuffed toys and some chew toys in the crate will help to keep the pup amused and will increase her enjoyment of the crate. A crate should not be used for more than one hour for a young puppy and should never be used for punishment.

Where you place the crate in your home is important for your dog's comfort. Keep it out of drafts and direct sunlight (for a wire crate,

a sheet or blanket can be used as a cover for privacy and draft protection, and removed when not needed). It is also very important that the crate be in a "people area," not in a place where the dog will be isolated from her family. Don't hesitate to move the crate to "where the action is" at any given time, such as the living room, the bedroom or the kitchen.

Choose a time to start training when the dog is ready for rest, after she has relieved herself and has had plenty of exercise. Begin by placing a piece of kibble in the crate so your dog will enter willingly and, in a cheerful tone of voice, use a command such as "kennel" or "crate." At first, keep the door open when the dog is inside. Then, after acclimating the dog to the crate with the door open, close the door for a few minutes. Be sure to give the dog some toys so that she has something to do. Gradually increase the time that the door is closed and practice leaving and returning to the room without any fuss. This matter-of-fact attitude helps to avoid separation anxiety later on. Your comings and goings should never be a big event with apologetic departures or excited greetings. Ignore any vocal

protest. Allow the dog out only after she has settled down and has accepted containment.

ACTIVITY

A Jack Russell Terrier is a body in motion; these dogs need exercise throughout their entire lives. Even in their senior years, they still tend to act like puppies—they just take longer naps!

Russell puppies will follow closely at your heels, even to the point of getting stepped on. They will wiggle when you hold them and, being as strong as they are, may wiggle right out of your grasp. Fearless by nature, they will launch themselves from dangerous heights, and must never be left where they can fall from chairs or sofas and be injured.

Physical and mental needs of the Jack Russell Terrier can be met in good part by making sure the dog has adequate exercise. Dedicate part of each day to taking your terrier on long walks. Playing ball may be good exercise, too, but a brisk walk goes a much longer way in meeting the needs of the dog. It is not easy to tire JRTs. Their need for activity cannot be compromised and many

behavioral problems can be alleviated by increased exercise.

IDENTIFICATION

Identification tags are easily lost and any collar can be removed. Other means of identification are much more reliable. Many dogs are tattooed on the inner thigh with the owner's social security number, which is registered with a reliable system like the National Dog Registry. Other owners prefer to have a microchip implanted beneath the dog's skin. Many dogs that would otherwise have been lost have found their way home because they were able to be positively identified.

13

Providing your JRT with a dog run outdoors is a good way to let her be active while you're away, but don't leave her there all day without toys—boredom will quickly lead to behavior problems.

PUPPY ESSENTIALS

Your new puppy will need:

food bowl	bed
water bowl	crate
collar	exercise pen
leash	toys
ID tag	grooming supplies

Even at an early age, JRTs are inclined to explore in search of adventure whether or not you are with them. It's easy to see why

Do yourself and your puppy a favor and put an ID tag on her as soon as you bring her home.

identification is so necessary for the adventurous and independent Jack Russell Terrier.

ROUTINE

A routine is helpful to all dogs. Upon rising, they need to relieve themselves and play, then go back to rest some more. After their morning nap, they are ready for more play and exercise, and then their afternoon nap. If you work at home, you have an ideal companion. If you work away from home, it is best if you can get back midday to spend some time with the dog, letting her out and playing with her. If your dog must be alone during the day, leave a radio on to keep her company and use gates to confine her to one or two rooms, but don't leave her alone for too many hours, and never leave her crated for more than a few hours at a time. This is especially hard for puppies, who may feel they are being punished or abandoned.

Perhaps a friend or neighbor can help by spending some time with the dog in the early afternoon, as JRTs really do cherish companionship. If you have no alternative but to be gone all day, and no one to help, you might want to consider waiting and getting a dog or puppy at a later time in your life. When you get home, take the dog outside immediately and later, after feeding and watering, take her on a long evening walk.

TOYS

Jack Russells love toys, and appropriate ones are necessary for all stages of their lives. Hard rubber toys, Kongs, Boomer Balls and Activity Balls are all good toys for your dog. Soft rubber squeaky toys can be hazardous and should be avoided.

Hard rubber balls are always a favorite and the ones with a channel cut through them are easy for little mouths to carry. Rope toys with hard rubber chew areas are very suitable and come in many shapes and sizes. Large, tightly rolled pieces of rawhide may be acceptable, but avoid smaller pieces that can be chewed down into bits and choke the dog.

By providing your JRT with proper, tough, terrier-safe toys, you can help to avoid damage to furniture and furnishings. Never allow your puppy or dog to chew on

anything that is not meant for that activity, and always be ready to provide her with a good toy as a substitute for whatever forbidden item might be in her mouth. In distracting the puppy from such negative behavior, be sure to praise her for accepting the substitution.

It is important to enroll in an obedience class with your Jack Russell Terrier. The training and communication that you build together will strengthen your relationship and help to establish you as her pack leader.

BRINGING HOME AN ADULT DOG

Many healthy, well-behaved, older JRTs are in need of new homes and can be applied for through the

Jack Russells love a good game of tug, and a rope toy like this one will give your puppy something appropriate to chew on.

15

Adult Jack Russell Terriers can make good pets too; consider adopting a grown JRT in need of a home.

JRTCA's Russell Rescue. By selecting an adult dog, you can get a pet that is already trained, friendly and relaxed.

An older dog entering your home and life for the first time has a history and habits, and may be more cautious in her new surroundings. The best thing you can do is to make the homecoming as stress-free as possible, and make your home a comfortable, stable environment in which your new dog will feel secure.

If you get a re-homed dog from a rescue group or other source, you may not know much about the dog's history. The more you can find out, the better prepared you will be for the task ahead. Unfortunately, some rescue dogs have been harmed at the hands of humans, and will have to be patiently taught to love and trust again.

You can make this easier by being sensitive to the special circumstances of your JRT. Notice anything that seems to make her uncomfortable. Avoid movements or noises that seem to scare her. Introduce children to your new JRT in as calm a manner as possible.

If you have another pet in the house, make sure their introduction and interactions are supervised, especially at first. It's best to introduce them outside on neutral territory, leashed of course. As they become more comfortable with each other, let them out together, but stay close. Do not leave them unsupervised until you are sure they have accepted each other.

Take your dog for long walks around your neighborhood to let her get her bearings and familiarize herself with her new environment. The sooner she feels at home, the better. An older JRT should adjust quickly to your home and lifestyle.

CHAPTER THREE

To Good Health

The strongest body and soundest genetic background will not help a dog lead a healthy life unless he receives regular attention from his owner. Dogs are susceptible to infections, parasites and diseases for which they have no natural immunity. It is up to us to take preventative measures to make sure that none of these interferes with our dog's health. It may help to think of the upkeep of a dog's health in relation to the calendar. Certain things need to be done on a weekly, monthly and annual basis.

PREVENTIVE HEALTH CARE

Weekly grooming can be the single best monitor of a dog's overall health. The actual condition of the coat and skin and the "feel" of the body can indicate good health or potential problems. Grooming will help you discover small lumps on or under the skin in the early stages

Run your hands regularly over your dog to feel for any injuries.

FIGHTING FLEAS

Remember, the fleas you see on your dog are only part of the problem—the smallest part! To rid your dog and home of fleas, you need to treat your dog *and* your home. Here's how:

- Identify where your pet(s) sleeps. These are "hot spots."

- Clean your pets' bedding regularly by vacuuming and washing.

- Spray "hot spots" with a nontoxic, long-lasting flea larvicide.

- Treat outdoor "hot spots" with insecticide.

- Kill eggs on pets with a product containing insect growth regulators (IGRs).

- Kill fleas on pets per your veterinarian's recommendation.

before they become large enough to be seen without close examination.

You may spot fleas and ticks when brushing the coat and examining the skin. Besides harboring diseases and parasites, they can make daily life a nightmare for some dogs. Many dogs are severely allergic to even a couple of fleas on their bodies. They scratch, chew and destroy their coat and skin because of fleas. Even if the fleas are not actually seen, their existence can be confirmed by small black specks in the coat.

Flea Control

Flea control is never a simple endeavor. Dogs bring fleas inside, where they lay eggs in the carpeting and furniture—anywhere your dog goes in the house. Consequently, real control is a matter of not only treating the dog but also the other environments the flea inhabits. The yard can be sprayed, and in the house, sprays and flea bombs can be used, but there are more choices for the dog. Flea sprays are effective for one to two weeks depending on their ingredients. Dips applied to the dog's coat following a bath have equal periods of effectiveness. The disadvantage to both of these is that some dogs may have problems with the chemicals.

Flea collars can be effective, as they prevent the fleas from traveling to your dog's head, where it's moister and more hospitable. Dog owners tend to leave flea collars on their dogs long after they've ceased to be effective. Again, some dogs may have problems with flea collars, and children should never be allowed to handle them.

Some owners opt for products that can work from the inside out. One is a pet-safe chemical that, when applied to a certain spot deep in the dog's coat, is absorbed into the dog's body and works for up to a month. Another such option is a pill (prescribed by a veterinarian) that you give to the dog on a regular basis in his food. The chemicals in the pill course through the dog's bloodstream, and when a flea bites, the blood kills the flea.

Going over a dog thoroughly every day with a flea comb works wonders. All you will need is a fine flea comb and a glass of water into which you have mixed a few drops of mild liquid soap. When the comb picks up fleas, quickly dip it into the soapy water and remove the fleas

The flea is a die-hard pest.

Three types of ticks (l-r): the wood tick, brown dog tick and deer tick.

Use tweezers to remove ticks from your dog.

from the comb. (The soap coats the flea and kills it.) Keep the glass close to you. If it is too far away, the flea may have time to jump off the comb.

As you examine your dog, check also for ticks that may have lodged in his skin, particularly around the ears or in the hair at the base of the ear, the armpits or around the

19

genitals. If you find a tick, which is a small insect about the size of a pencil eraser when engorged with blood, smear it with Vaseline. As the tick suffocates, it will back out and you can then grab it with tweezers and kill it. If the tick doesn't back out, grab it with tweezers and slowly pull it out, twisting very gently. Don't just grab and pull or the tick's head may separate from the body. If the head remains in the skin, an infection or abscess may result and veterinary treatment may be required.

A word of caution: Don't use your fingers or fingernails to pull out ticks. Ticks can carry a number of diseases, including Lyme disease, Rocky Mountain spotted fever and others, all of which can be very serious.

Proper Ear Care

Another weekly job is cleaning the ears. Many times an ear problem is evident if a dog scratches his ears or shakes his head frequently. Clean ears are less likely to develop problems, and if something does occur, it will be spotted while it can be treated easily. If a dog's ears are very dirty and seem to need cleaning on a daily basis, it is a good indication that something else is going on in the ears besides ordinary dirt and the normal accumulation of earwax. A visit to the veterinarian may indicate a situation that needs special medication.

Brushing Teeth

Regular brushing of the teeth often does not seem necessary when a dog is young and spends much of his time chewing; the teeth always seem to be immaculately clean. As a dog ages, it becomes more important to brush the teeth daily.

Cleaning your dog's ears every week or two with a cotton swab and ear cleanser will help keep them healthy and free of infection.

To help prolong the health of your dog's mouth, he should have his teeth cleaned twice a year at a veterinary clinic. Observing the mouth regularly, checking for the formation of abnormalities or broken teeth, can lead to early detection of oral cancer or infection.

Keeping Nails Trimmed

The nails on all feet should be kept short enough so they do not touch the ground when the dog walks.

Dogs with long nails can have difficulty walking on hard or slick surfaces. This can be especially true of older dogs. As nails grow longer, the only way the foot can compensate and retain balance is for the toes themselves to spread apart, causing the foot itself to become flattened and splayed.

Nails that are allowed to become long are also more prone to splitting. This is painful to the dog and usually requires surgical removal of the remainder of the nail for proper healing to occur.

Keeping Eyes Clear

Eye care is important, and eyes should be checked every week, or

Check your dog's teeth frequently and brush them regularly.

21

Squeeze eye ointment into the lower lid.

more often if the dog is working. When a Jack Russell Terrier follows his nose and instincts, he will go to ground and probably end up with dirt or particles of sand in his eyes. If this foreign matter is not removed, the corneas may be scratched. Even non-working dogs will often have foreign matter in their eyes. You can wash out the eyes with lukewarm water or a special eye-cleaning preparation. Pull the lids back to make sure there is no dirt hiding in the corners of the eye.

Excessive tearing can be an indication that a tear duct is blocked. This can be corrected by a simple surgical procedure. Eye discharge that is thicker and mucous-like in consistency is often a sign of some type of eye infection or actual injury to the eye. This can be verified by a veterinarian, who will provide a topical ointment to place in the corner of the eye. Most minor eye injuries heal quickly if proper action is taken.

VACCINES

All dogs need yearly vaccinations to protect them from common deadly diseases. The DHL vaccine, which protects a dog from distemper, hepatitis and leptospirosis, is given for the first time at about 7 weeks of age, followed by one or two boosters several weeks apart. After this, a dog should be vaccinated every year throughout his life.

Since the mid-1970s, parvovirus and coronavirus have been the cause of death for thousands of dogs. Puppies and older dogs are most frequently affected by these illnesses. Fortunately, vaccines for these are now routinely given on a yearly basis in combination with the DHL shot.

Kennel cough, though rarely dangerous in a healthy dog that receives proper treatment, can be annoying. It can be picked up anywhere that large numbers of dogs congregate, such as veterinary clinics, grooming shops, boarding kennels, obedience classes and dog shows. The Bordatella vaccine, given twice a year, will protect a dog from getting most strains of kennel cough. It is often not routinely given, so it may be necessary to request it.

INTERNAL PARASITES

While the exterior part of a dog's body hosts fleas and ticks, the inside of the body is commonly inhabited by a variety of parasites. Most of these are in the worm family. Tapeworms, roundworms, whipworms, hookworms and heartworm all plague our dogs. There are also several types of protozoa, mainly *coccidia* and *giardia*, that cause problems.

The common tapeworm is acquired by the dog eating infected

Vaccinations help protect your puppy from a number of common canine diseases.

fleas. Normally one is not aware that a healthy dog even has tapeworms. The only clues may be a dull coat, a loss of weight despite a good appetite or occasional gastrointestinal problems. Confirmation is by the presence of worm segments in the stool. These appear as small, pinkish-white, flattened rectangular-shaped pieces. When dry, they look like rice. If segments are not present, diagnosis can be made by the discovery of eggs when a stool sample is examined under a microscope. Ridding a dog temporarily of tapeworm is easy with a worming medicine prescribed by a veterinarian. Over-the-counter wormers are not effective for tapeworms and may be dangerous. Long-term tapeworm control is not possible unless the flea situation is also addressed.

YOUR PUPPY'S VACCINES

Vaccines are given to prevent your dog from getting an infectious disease like canine distemper or rabies. Vaccines are the ultimate preventive medicine: They're given before your dog ever gets the disease so as to protect him from the disease. That's why it is necessary for your dog to be vaccinated routinely. Your veterinarian will put your puppy on a proper schedule and will remind you when to bring in your dog for shots.

Ascarids are the most common roundworm (nematode) found in dogs. Adult dogs that have round-worms rarely exhibit any symptoms that would indicate the worm is in their body. These worms are cylindrical in shape and may be as long as 4 to 5 inches. They do pose a real danger to puppies, where they are usually passed from the mother through the uterus to the unborn puppies.

It is wise to assume that all puppies have roundworms. In heavy infestations they will actually appear in the puppy stools, though their presence is best diagnosed by a stool sample. Treatment is easy and can begin as early as 2 weeks of age and is administered every two weeks thereafter until eggs no longer appear in a stool sample or dead worms are not found in the stool following treatment. Severely infected puppies can die from roundworm infestation. Again, the

worming medication should be obtained through a veterinarian.

Hookworm is usually found in warmer climates and infestation is generally from ingestion of larvae from the ground or penetration of the skin by larvae. Hookworms can cause anemia, diarrhea and emaciation. As these worms are very tiny and not visible to the eye, their diagnosis must be made by a veterinarian.

Whipworms live in the large intestine and cause few if any symptoms. Dogs usually become infected when they ingest larvae in contaminated soil. Again, diagnosis and treatment should all be done by a veterinarian. One of the easiest ways to control these parasites is by picking up stools on a daily basis. This will help prevent the soil from becoming infested.

The protozoa can be trickier to diagnose and treat. Coccidiosis and giardia are the most common, and primarily affect young puppies. They are generally associated with overcrowded, unsanitary conditions and can be acquired from the mother (if she is a carrier), the premises themselves (soil) or even water, especially rural puddles and streams.

Common internal parasites (l-r): roundworm, whipworm, tapeworm and hookworm.

The most common symptom of protozoan infection is mucous-like blood-tinged feces. It is only with freshly collected samples that diagnosis of this condition can be made. With coccidiosis, besides diarrhea, the puppies will appear listless and lose their appetites. Puppies often harbor the protozoa and show no symptoms unless placed under stress. Consequently, many times a puppy will not become ill until he goes to his new home. Once diagnosed, treatment is quick and effective and the puppy returns to normal almost immediately.

Heartworm

The most serious of the common internal parasites is the heartworm. A dog that is bitten by a mosquito infected with the heartworm *microfilaria* (larvae) will develop worms that are 6 to 12 inches long. As these worms mature they take up residence in the dog's heart.

The symptoms of heartworm may include coughing, tiring easily, difficulty breathing and weight loss. Heart failure and liver disease may eventually result. Verification of heartworm infection is done by drawing blood and screening for the microfilaria.

In areas where heartworm is a risk, it is best to place a dog on a preventative, usually a pill given once a month.

At least once a year a dog should have a full veterinary examination. The overall condition of the dog can be observed and a blood sample collected for a complete yearly screening. This way the dog's thyroid functions can be tested, and the job the dog's organs are doing can be monitored. If there are any problems, this form of testing can spot trouble areas while they are easily treatable.

Proper care, regular vaccinations, periodic stool checks and preventative medications for such things as heartworm will all help ensure your dog's health.

SPAYING/ NEUTERING

Spaying a female dog or neutering a male is another way to make sure they lead long and healthy lives. Females spayed at a young age have almost no risk of developing mammary tumors or reproductive

25

problems. Neutering a male is an excellent solution to dog aggression and also removes the chances of testicular cancer.

There is absolutely no benefit to a female having a first season before being spayed, nor in letting her have a litter. The decision to breed any dog should always be taken seriously. The obvious considerations are whether he or she is a good physical specimen of the breed and has a sound temperament. There are several genetic problems that are common to Jack Russell Terriers, such as patella luxation, Legg-Perthes disease and deafness. Responsible breeders screen for

these prior to making breeding decisions.

Finding suitable homes for puppies is another serious consideration. Due to their popularity, many people are attracted to JRTs and seek puppies without realizing the drawbacks of the breed.

Owning a dog is a lifetime commitment to that animal. There are so many unwanted dogs—and yes, even unwanted Jack Russell Terriers—that people must be absolutely sure that they are not just adding to the pet overpopulation problem. When breeding a litter of puppies, it is more likely that you will lose more than you

There is no evidence to support the myth that it is beneficial to a dog's health if she has a litter of puppies.

will make, when time, effort, equipment and veterinary costs are factored in.

COMMON PROBLEMS

Lameness

A limp that appears from nowhere and gets progressively worse is cause for concern. The first thing to do is try to ascertain where the problem actually is. Check the legs and feet for any areas of tenderness, swelling or infection. There are numerous possibilities to consider.

In the JRT, patella luxation or Legg-Perthes disease may be the problem. These maladies are discussed later in this chapter. Hip dysplasia is a problem in all dogs, although it is not particularly common in the Jack Russell. As a dog ages these joints wear down, and eventually arthritis is associated with the disease. Hip dysplasia can only be properly diagnosed by x-ray.

Anytime a dog or puppy becomes lame and rest is prescribed as treatment, it is essential to keep that dog almost completely inactive, except for potty visits, until the injury heals.

ADVANTAGES OF SPAY/NEUTER

The greatest advantage of spaying (for females) or neutering (for males) your dog is that you are guaranteed your dog will not produce puppies. There are too many puppies already available for too few homes. There are other advantages as well.

Advantages of Spaying

No messy heats.

No "suitors" howling at your windows or waiting in your yard.

Prevents pyometra (disease of the uterus) and decreases incidence of breast cancer.

Advantages of Neutering

Decreases fights, but doesn't affect the dog's personality.

Decreases roaming.

Decreased incidences of urogenital diseases.

Not Eating or Vomiting

One of the surest signs that a dog may be ill is if he does not eat. This is why it is important to know your dog's eating habits. For most dogs one missed meal under normal conditions is not cause for alarm, but more than that and it is time to take

27

WHEN TO CALL
THE VETERINARIAN

In any emergency situation, you should call your veterinarian immediately. You can make the difference in your dog's life by staying as calm as possible when you call and by giving the doctor or the assistant as much information as possible before you leave for the clinic. That way, the vet will be able to take immediate, specific action to remedy your dog's situation.

Emergencies include acute abdominal pain, suspected poisoning, snakebite, burns, frostbite, shock, dehydration, abnormal vomiting or bleeding and deep wounds. You are the best judge of your dog's health, as you live with and observe him every day. Don't hesitate to call your veterinarian if you suspect trouble.

your dog to the veterinarian to search for reasons. The vital signs should be checked and gums examined. Normally a dog's gums are pink; if ill they will be pale and gray.

There are many reasons why dogs vomit, and many of them are not cause for alarm. You should be concerned, however, when your dog vomits frequently over the period of a day. If the vomiting is associated with diarrhea, elevated temperature and lethargy, the cause is most likely a virus. The dog should receive supportive veterinary treatment if recovery is to proceed quickly. Vomiting that is not associated with other symptoms is often an indication of an intestinal blockage. Rocks, toys and clothing can lodge in a dog's intestine, preventing the normal passage of digested foods and liquids.

If a blockage is suspected, the first thing to do is an x-ray of the stomach and intestinal region. Sometimes objects will pass on their own, but often surgical removal of the object is necessary.

Diarrhea

Diarrhea is characterized as very loose to watery stools that a dog has difficulty controlling. It can be caused by anything as simple as changing diet, overeating, eating rich human food or having internal parasites.

First try to locate the source of the problem and remove it from the dog's access. Immediate relief is usually available by giving the dog an intestinal relief medication such as Kaopectate or Pepto-Bismol. Use the same amount per weight as for humans. Take the dog off his food for a day to allow the intestines to rest, then feed meals of cooked rice with bland ingredients added. Gradually add the dog's regular food back into his diet.

If diarrhea is bloody or has a more offensive odor than might be expected and is combined with vomiting and fever, it is most likely a virus and requires immediate veterinary attention. If worms are suspected as the cause, a stool sample should be examined by a veterinarian and treatment to rid the dog of the parasite should follow when the dog is back to normal. If allergies are suspected, a series of tests can be given to find the cause. This is especially likely if, after recovery and no other evidence of a cause exists, a dog returns to his former diet and the diarrhea recurs.

Bloat

Another problem associated with the gastrointestinal system is bloat, or acute gastric dilatation. It most commonly occurs in large adult dogs that eat large amounts of dry kibble. Exercise or excessive amounts of water consumed immediately following a meal can trigger the condition.

In a dog with bloat, the abdominal area will appear swollen, and the area will be painful. In severe cases the stomach actually twists on itself and a condition called torsion occurs. If you suspect that your dog is suffering from bloat, run your dog to the nearest veterinary clinic immediately.

Seizures

Seizures vary in severity from trembling and stiffness to frenzied, rapid movements of the legs, foaming at the mouth and loss of urine and bowel movements. The latter is usually considered a grand mal seizure.

Seizures are caused by electrical activity in the brain, and there are many reasons why they may occur. Ingestion of some poisons, such as strychnine and insecticides, will cause seizures. These are generally long lasting and severe in nature. Injuries to the skull, tumors and cancers can trigger seizures.

If there appears to be no reason for the seizure it is possible the cause is congenital epilepsy. This is particularly true if a dog is under the age of 3. From the age of 5, dogs are prone to develop old age onset epilepsy, which also may have a genetic predisposition.

IDENTIFYING YOUR DOG

It's a terrible thing to think about, but your dog could somehow, someday, get lost or stolen. How would you get him back? Your best bet would be to have some form of identification on your dog. You can choose from a collar and tags, a tattoo, a microchip or a combination of these three.

Every dog should wear a buckle collar with identification tags. They are the quickest and easiest way for a stranger to identify your dog. It's best to inscribe the tags with your name and phone number; you don't need to include your dog's name.

There are two ways to permanently identify your dog. The first is a tattoo, placed on the inside of your dog's thigh. The tattoo should be your social security number or your dog's AKC registration number.

The second is a microchip, a rice-grain-sized pellet that's inserted under the dog's skin at the base of the neck, between the shoulder blades. When a scanner is passed over the dog, it will beep, notifying the person that the dog has a chip. The scanner will then show a code, identifying the dog. Microchips are becoming more and more popular and are certainly the wave of the future.

Never try to touch or move a dog during a seizure. If there is anything nearby that might be knocked over by their flailing legs and could injure them, move it out of the way. If the seizure does not stop within five minutes, call your veterinarian.

Even after a typical seizure, your vet may suggest you bring your dog in for an examination and blood work. If a cause is not found, the best course is usually to wait and see if your dog has another seizure. If a dog only has seizures once or twice a year there is no reason to place him on preventive medication. If seizures occur on a regular basis and are of the same nature each time, the dog is considered to have epilepsy and medication should be considered.

In typical epilepsy, a dog may act restless, weird, stare and bark for some time before the actual seizure. The seizure itself lasts several minutes. A second seizure can be triggered by turning a light on or by moving the dog as he is recovering.

If seizures are infrequent and mild, an epileptic dog can lead a fairly normal life. Owners will generally begin to see a pattern in the time of day the seizures occur and their frequency, and can plan their dog's activities accordingly.

Coughing

Throughout the day most dogs will cough to get something out of their throats and it is usually ignored. If coughing persists, then it is time to look for causes.

Applying abdominal thrusts can save a choking dog.

A common cause for a dry hacking cough is kennel cough, which is contagious and usually picked up through association with other dogs. A dog with kennel cough should receive veterinary attention and be placed on antibiotics and a cough suppressant. During treatment and recovery, the dog should be kept indoors and warm as much as possible. Kennel cough, if not cared for properly, can easily turn into pneumonia in cold conditions. Infected dogs should be isolated from other dogs until they have recovered.

Chronic coughing after exercise can also be a sign of heart failure, especially in an older dog. It may also indicate a heartworm infection. If this occurs regularly, consult your veterinarian.

Most changes in the breathing pattern of a healthy dog, such as rapid inhalations or panting, are caused by exercise, stress and heat. If a dog is having problems breathing and it is also accompanied by

coughing or gagging, it may be a sign that an air passage is blocked. Check for an object lodged in your dog's throat. If you can't remove it yourself, use the Heimlich maneuver. Place your dog on his side and, using both hands palms down, apply quick thrusts to the abdomen, just below the dog's last rib. If your dog won't lie down, grasp either side of the end of the rib cage and squeeze in short thrusts. Make a sharp enough movement to cause the air in the lungs to force the object out. If the cause cannot be found or removed, then professional help is needed.

Shallow breathing can be a result of an injury to the ribs or a lung problem. A wheezing noise that can be heard as a dog breathes is an indication of a serious problem. If other symptoms include a fever and lethargy, the problem may be associated with a lung disease. The symptoms may indicate treatment for an infection. An x-ray will confirm the presence of a growth or infection in the lungs.

Sometimes a dog exhibits no greater signs that something is different than increased lethargy, weight gain and even a poor coat. It may be time to consider checking the dog's thyroid levels for a possible hypothyroid condition. Low thyroid most commonly results in a poor coat and skin and eventual infertility in an intact male or female. A thyroid test will indicate what thyroid levels are low and whether daily thyroid medication should be given.

Skin Problems

Certain skin conditions should not be ignored if home treatment is not working. For example, if a dog is so sensitive and allergic to fleas that his coat and skin are literally destroyed by chewing, it is time to seek help. Cortisone can help relieve the itching and stop the dog from destroying himself, but it has side effects, too! It's best to get your vet's advice.

Mange is caused by tiny mites that live on the dog's skin. The most common types are sarcoptic and demodetic mange. Diagnosis must

be made by a veterinarian because the mites are too small to be seen.

Sarcoptic mange first occurs as small red bumps on the dog's skin and causes intense itching. If allowed to continue there is hair loss from chewing, and the affected skin becomes crusty, especially around the muzzle, elbows and hocks.

The mite that causes demodetic mange lives in the pores of the skin of most dogs. Certain conditions cause the dog's natural immunity to this mite to break down, and the result is patches of hair loss, usually around the nose or eyes. There is no itching associated with this condition and it primarily occurs in dogs under 1 year of age. If treated properly the hair returns to normal. In the generalized form of the disease, hair loss occurs in large patches all over the body. Obviously this is a much more serious condition.

Hot spots are one of the most baffling skin problems. They can be caused by a number of things, including flea bites and allergies. A warm, moist, infected area on the skin appears out of nowhere and can be several inches large. At home one should clip the hair around it, then clean it with an antiseptic and dilute (3 percent hydrogen peroxide). Spraying with a topical anaesthetic immediately relieves itching. Topical ointments can also help. If the spot is not healing and appears to be getting larger or infected, veterinary help should be sought.

A similar type of skin condition is the lick sore. These sores are almost always on the lower part of the front legs or tops of the feet. A dog will lick a spot and out of boredom continue licking it until the hair is gone and the skin is hard, red and shiny. The sore will heal on its own if kept clean and the dog is prevented access to it by an anti-chewing spray or by wearing an Elizabethan collar.

Tumors

As dogs age they are more apt to develop various types of tumors. Fatty tumors grow just under the dog's skin and are not attached to anything. These are usually benign accumulations of fatty cells. If you see or feel any such lumps on your dog, you should consult your veterinarian. Tumors and bumps that appear and grow rapidly, are

strange in color or appearance or are attached to the bone should receive immediate attention.

Cuts and Wounds

Any cut over $\frac{1}{2}$ inch in length should be stitched for it to heal. Small cuts usually heal by themselves if they are rinsed well, washed with an antibiotic soap and checked regularly with further cleansing of soap or a hydrogen peroxide solution. When they occur in areas that are exposed to dirt, such as the feet, it may be advisable to place a wrap on the injury, but it should be removed frequently. If signs of infection appear, such as swelling, redness or warmth, it should be looked at by a veterinarian.

33

An Elizabethan collar keeps your dog from licking a fresh wound.

Puncture wounds should never be bandaged or stitched. They occur most commonly from bites, nails or wires. Anytime it is suspected that a dog might have been pierced by a nail or bitten, the body should be carefully examined for such wounds. As they often do not bleed very much they can be difficult to spot. If not treated, they can result in infection or even conditions as dangerous as tetanus.

If the wound is discovered within a short time of the occurrence, try to make it bleed by applying pressure around it. Flush it with water, then clean it with soap. Leave it exposed so that oxygen is able to stay in the wound and prevent an anaerobic condition from developing. Place a dilute hydrogen peroxide on it several times a day. Watch it carefully for any indications of infection. Anytime your dog is injured, consider placing him on an antibiotic to prevent infection.

GIVING MEDICATION

When a dog has been diagnosed with a problem that requires medication it is usually in the form of a pill or liquid. Because it is essential for a dog to have the entire pill or capsule in order for the dosage to be effective, it's necessary to actually give the dog the pill rather than mix it in his food or wrap it in meat, which can be chewed up and spit out. Open your dog's mouth and place the pill on the back of the middle of his tongue. Then hold his head up with his mouth held shut and stroke his throat. When the dog swallows, you can let go.

Liquid medication is most easily given in a syringe. These are usually marked so the amount is accurately measured. Hold the dog's head upward at about 45°, open the mouth slightly and place the end of the syringe in the area in the back of the mouth between the cheek and rear molars. Hold your dog's mouth shut until he swallows.

If your dog needs eye medication, apply it by pulling down the lower eyelid and placing the ointment on the inside of the lid. Then close the eye and gently disperse the solution around the eye. Eye drops can be placed directly on the eye. Giving ear medicine is similar to cleaning the ears. The drops are placed in the canal and the ear is then massaged.

COMMON JACK RUSSELL TERRIER PROBLEMS

Some genetic problems have been found in Jack Russells, but, fortunately, fewer than are found in some other breeds. Dogs with known defects should not be bred.

To give a pill, open the mouth wide, then drop it in the back of the throat.

35

PATELLA LUXATION Patella luxation is the equivalent of a slipped kneecap in humans. When the kneecap (patella) becomes dislocated, there may be pain and difficulty straightening the knee. The luxation may be permanent or it may be intermittent, with the kneecap popping in and out of position. The dog may move in a normal manner one minute and be lame the next.

This condition can lead to the premature development of arthritis and restricted, painful movement. If the condition becomes acute, corrective surgery is the preferred treatment, and patients usually recover fully.

ATAXIA Ataxia is a disorder of either the muscles or limbs. If a Jack Russell Terrier has a mild case, he may simply move awkwardly. In a

more advanced case, the dog will have difficulty in maintaining his balance—in a severe case, the dog will be unable to stand or walk.

LEGG-PERTHES DISEASE This disease is often seen in small dogs. It is caused by destruction of the ball-and-socket hip join. Permanent arthritis may be a result of Legg-Perthes.

MYASTHENIA GRAVIS This disease affects the dog's motor nerves and is evidenced by a weakness in the hindquarters. A JRT with this disease may have trouble getting up from a sitting position and will move in a staggering fashion.

LENS LUXATION Lens luxation is a dislocation of the lens, usually appearing during a dog's middle age. It is an inherited disease of the

Use a scarf to make a temporary muzzle, as shown.

tissues that hold the lens in place. Both eyes are usually affected and secondary glaucoma may result. Surgery will remove the affected lens or lenses. Vision after surgery will be reduced but still be present, whereas glaucoma will eventually destroy vision altogether. This treatment, while not perfect, is certainly preferable to ensuing blindness.

HERNIAS   A hernia is a protrusion of an organ or tissue through a body wall. In JRTs, umbilical and inguinal hernias are passed on genetically.

DEAFNESS   Deafness occurs often in white-coated dogs. The dog may be totally deaf (bilateral) or deaf in only one ear (unilateral). Unilateral deafness is more difficult to detect as the dog quickly learns to compensate for his loss in the one deaf ear.

It takes a very dedicated owner with special abilities to provide for the protection and safety of a totally deaf Jack Russell. Some have fared quite well living with hearing dogs, or with deaf people who have taught the dog sign language. But there are also reported incidents of biting which have occurred as a result of an exaggerated startle response from a profoundly deaf dog.

FIRST AID AND EMERGENCIES

While we never plan on emergencies happening, we can be partially prepared by knowing which veterinary clinics are open if something occurs at night or on the weekend. Telephone numbers should be posted so they can be easily located. First-aid measures can be taken to help ensure that your dog gets to a veterinarian in time for treatment to be effective.

Anytime a dog is in extreme pain, even the most docile one may bite if touched. As a precaution, the dog's mouth should be restrained with some type of muzzle. A rope, pair of pantyhose or strip of cloth about 2 feet long all work in a pinch.

First tie a loose knot that has an opening large enough to easily fit around the dog's nose. Once it is on, tighten the knot on the top of the muzzle. Then bring the two ends down and tie another knot underneath the dog's chin. Finally, pull the ends behind the head and tie a knot below the ears. Don't

do this if there is an injury to the head or the dog requires artificial respiration.

If a dog has been injured or is too ill to walk on his own he will have to carried to be moved. It is important to be very careful when this is done to prevent further injury or trauma. Keep the dog's body as flat and still as possible. A blanket can work if all four corners are held taut. A piece of plywood or extremely stiff cardboard works best, if available.

ARTIFICIAL RESPIRATION

Artificial respiration is necessary if breathing has stopped. Situations that may cause a state of

Because your Jack Russell Terrier will inevitably take some risks during his lifetime, you'll want to be familiar with basic first-aid procedures for dogs.

unconsciousness include drowning, choking, electric shock or even shock itself. If you've taken a course in human CPR you will discover that similar methods are used on dogs. The first thing to do is check the mouth and air passages for any object that might obstruct breathing. If you find nothing, or when it is cleared, hold the dog's mouth while covering the nose completely with your mouth. Gently exhale into the dog's nose. This should be done at between ten to twelve breaths per minute.

If the heart has stopped beating, place the dog on his right side and place the palm of your hand on the rib cage just behind the elbows. Press down six times and then wait five seconds and repeat. This should be done in conjunction with artificial respiration, so it will require two people. Artificial respiration should be continued until the dog breathes on his own or the heart beats. Heart massage should continue until the heart beats on its own or no beat is felt for five minutes.

SHOCK Whenever a dog is injured or is seriously ill, the odds are good that he will go into a state of shock. A dog in shock will be listless, weak and cold to the touch. His gums will be pale. If not treated, a dog will die from shock, even if the illness or injuries themselves are not fatal. The conditions of the dog should continue to be treated, but the dog should be kept as comfortable as possible. A blanket can help keep the dog warm. A dog in shock needs immediate veterinary care.

SEVERE BLEEDING When severe bleeding from a cut occurs the area should be covered with bandaging material or a clean cloth and should have pressure applied to it. If it appears that an artery is involved and the wound is on a limb, then a tourniquet should be applied. This can be made of a piece of cloth, gauze or sock if nothing else is available. It should be tied above the wound and checked every few minutes to make sure it is not so tight that circulation to the rest of the limb is cut off.

FRACTURE If a fracture is felt or suspected, the dog should be moved and transported as carefully as possible to a veterinarian. Attempting to treat a break at home can cause more damage than leaving it alone.

POISONING In the case of poisoning the only thing to do is get help immediately. If you know the source of the poison, take the container or object with you, as this may aid treatment.

In acidic or alkaline poisonings the chemicals must be neutralized. Pepto-Bismol or milk of magnesia at 2 teaspoons per 5 pounds of weight can be given for acids. Vinegar diluted at one part to four parts water at the same dosage can relieve alkaline poisons.

HEATSTROKE Heatstroke occurs when a dog's body temperature greatly exceeds the normal 101.5°. It can be caused by overexercise in warm temperatures, or if a dog is left in a closed vehicle for any period of time. A dog should *never* be left in an unventilated, unshaded vehicle. Even if you only plan to be gone for a minute, that time can unexpectedly increase and place a dog in a life-threatening situation.

Dogs suffering from heatstroke will feel hot to the touch and inhale short, shallow, rapid breaths. The heartbeat will be very fast. The dog must be cooled immediately, preferably being wet down with cool water in any way that is available. The dog

A First-Aid Kit

Keep a canine first-aid kit on hand for general care and emergencies. Check it periodically to make sure liquids haven't spilled or dried up, and replace medications and materials after they're used. Your kit should include:

- Activated charcoal tablets
- Adhesive tape (1 and 2 inches wide)
- Antibacterial ointment (for skin and eyes)
- Aspirin (buffered or enteric coated, *not* Ibuprofen)
- Bandages: gauze rolls (1 and 2 inches wide) and dressing pads
- Cotton balls
- Diarrhea medicine
- Dosing syringe
- Hydrogen peroxide (3%)
- Petroleum jelly
- Rectal thermometer
- Rubber gloves
- Rubbing alcohol
- Scissors
- Tourniquet
- Towel
- Tweezers

39

Some of the many household substances harmful to your dog.

should be wrapped in cool, damp towels and taken to the veterinarian immediately.

The opposite of heatstroke is hypothermia. When a dog is exposed to extreme cold for long periods of time his body temperature drops, he becomes chilled and he can go into shock. The dog should be placed in a warm environment and wrapped in towels or blankets. If the dog is already wet, a warm bath can help. Massaging the body will help increase the circulation to normal levels.

INSECT BITES

The seriousness of reactions to insect bites varies. The affected area will be red, swollen and painful. In the case of bee stings the stinger should always be removed. A paste made of baking soda and water can be applied to the wound and ice applied to the area for the relief of swelling. The bites of some spiders, centipedes and scorpions can cause severe illness and lead to shock.

CHAPTER FOUR

Positively Nutritious

Good nutrition is essential to good health, and the nutritional needs of a dog change throughout her life.

FEEDING YOUR JACK RUSSELL PUPPY

By the time you bring your puppy home she should be fully weaned and eagerly crunching on puppy kibble. The breeder should send you home with a supply of the food that the pup has been eating. You can either continue feeding that food or change to a different one. If you change, do it gradually, starting with about 25 percent of the new food, increasing the proportion for about a week until only the new food is being served. Changing food for dogs of any age should be done in this manner to avoid upsetting the puppy's or dog's digestive system.

Young puppies should be fed three times a day, at about the same times each day, one-third of the daily ration at each serving. Offer the food to the pup and allow her to eat for ten or fifteen minutes. At the end of that time, pick up the dish

TYPES OF FOODS/TREATS

There are three types of commercially available dog food—dry, canned and semi-moist—and a huge assortment of treats (lucky dogs!) to feed your dog. Which should you choose?

Dry and canned foods contain similar ingredients. The primary difference between them is their moisture content. The moisture is not just water. It's blood and broth, too, the very things that dogs adore. So while canned food is more palatable, dry food is more economical, convenient and effective in controlling tartar buildup. Most owners feed a 25 percent canned/75 percent dry diet to give their dogs the benefit of both. Just be sure your dog is getting the nutrition she needs (you and your veterinarian can determine this).

Semi-moist foods have the flavor dogs love and the convenience owners want. However, they tend to contain excessive amounts of artificial colors and preservatives.

Dog treats come in every size, shape and flavor imaginable, from organic cookies shaped like postmen to beefy chew sticks. Dogs seem to love them all, so enjoy the variety. Just be sure not to overindulge your dog and remember to account for snacks in your dog's daily calorie intake.

and do not offer more food until the next mealtime. You probably won't have to worry about your Jack Russell puppy eating enough—most are eager eaters. They may play around or even miss a meal or two, particularly when they are first brought to their new home, but they will soon get with the program. (A loss of appetite for longer periods may require your veterinarian's attention.) Be very sure that plenty of fresh, clean water is always available.

Puppies require more protein and calories per pound of body weight than adults, so a general rule of thumb for Jack Russells is to serve a pup a high-protein puppy chow. For the most part, this would be about 1 cup of good-quality, small kibble per day. You can check with the breeder for information on how much food he or she expects your pup will require as an adult. Feeding guidelines printed on dog-food bags are only estimates and should not be relied on as the precise amounts to feed your dog or puppy.

When your puppy reaches 5 or 6 months of age she can be fed

just twice a day, morning and evening, one-half the daily ration each.

FEEDING THE OLDER JACK RUSSELL

Jack Russells remain quite active well into their senior years. However, compared to the levels they maintained as youngsters, even these lively terriers tend to slow down and nap more as they age, perhaps gaining some weight in the process.

When JRTs get to be more than 6 years old they will require much less protein, and may require fewer calories (particularly if they are gaining some weight) while still needing all of the essential nutritional elements found in a well-balanced food. Feed your senior JRT smaller, more frequent meals of dog food designed for older dogs.

FEEDING MORE THAN ONE JRT

If you are feeding more than one puppy or dog, it is best to keep them

separated (perhaps serving them in their individual crates). By doing so, you can ensure that each dog gets to eat her full portion. Remove any food that has not been eaten within ten or fifteen minutes.

Make sure puppies don't get pushed aside by overeager bowl-mates.

43

TO SUPPLEMENT OR NOT TO SUPPLEMENT?

If you're feeding your dog a diet that's correct for her developmental stage and she's alert, healthy-looking and neither over- nor underweight, you don't need to add supplements. These include table scraps as well as vitamins and minerals. In fact, a growing puppy is in danger of developing musculoskeletal disorders by oversupplementation. If you have any concerns about the nutritional quality of the food you're feeding, discuss them with your veterinarian.

How to Read
the Dog-Food Label

With so many choices on the market, how can you be sure you are feeding the right food for your dog? The information is all there on the label—if you know what you're looking for.

Look for the nutritional claim right up top. Is the food "100% nutritionally complete"? If so, it's for nearly all life stages; "growth and maintenance," on the other hand, is for early development; puppy foods are marked as such, as are foods for senior dogs.

Ingredients are listed in descending order by weight. The first three or four ingredients will tell you the bulk of what the food contains. Look for the highest-quality ingredients, like meats and grains, to be among them.

The guaranteed analysis tells you what levels of protein, fat, fiber and moisture are in the food, in that order. While these numbers are meaningful, they won't tell you much about the quality of the food. Nutritional value is in the dry matter, not the moisture content.

In many ways, seeing is believing. If your dog has bright eyes, a shiny coat, a good appetite and a good energy level, chances are her diet's fine. Your dog's breeder and your veterinarian are good sources of advice if you're still confused.

Keeping Fit

JRTs should always appear fit and be in good working condition. All calories do count. Be sure to include biscuits and treats when calculating your dog's total daily intake. A good, quick way to determine if your terrier is carrying too much fat is to put your hand over her back, thumb on one side, fingers on the other, and run your hand lightly down the back. You should be able to feel the individual ribs, but you should not be able to see them.

What to Feed
Your JRT

Dry food, or primarily dry food, is recommended. With the kibble, some warm water may be added to release more food odors. Canned foods are not always necessary but, if you feel you must add it, take care that it does not exceed 20 or 25 percent of the dog's diet. A puppy raised on dry food, with or without the occasional addition of water, will be quite content with that food for her lifetime.

To help keep your dog's teeth and gums healthy, do avoid

44

semi-moist food and too much canned food. These soft preparations encourage tartar buildup, which can lead to periodontal disease. Hard kibble helps to keep teeth clean and gums healthy.

Premium food of high quality should always be chosen over less expensive food that may contain fillers and artificial colors and additives.

Supplements

One more consideration is supplements. Don't give them unless they are prescribed by your veterinarian for some special reason. All good-quality dog foods labeled as "complete" will provide all that your dog needs in the way of nutrition. Casual supplementation can cause serious imbalances and unexpected problems.

Basically, the food you serve your Jack Russell Terrier should contain protein, fat, carbohydrates, fiber, vitamins and minerals, all in proper quantities and in proper proportion to each other. It is highly unlikely that the quality food you purchase at your grocery or feed store will be lacking in any nutrient your dog

needs for healthy growth, development and maintenance.

Snacks

Good "people food" snacks for your terrier, in moderation, are pieces of carrot or apple. Most JRTs love them. Offer the snack between meals—yours and the dog's—or as rewards in training sessions. An easy guideline to remember is that if a food is good for you, it's also a healthy treat for your dog. In giving treats factor them into your plan for your JRT's daily calorie intake.

Most vets will recommend that canned food not exceed 25 percent of your dog's daily diet.

45

CHAPTER FIVE

Putting on the Dog

This chapter outlines procedures for the thorough care and grooming of your terrier's coat. However, the average dog will do just as well with basic grooming, together with proper care of the nails and feet and attention to health matters.

The real object is to get your hands on your dog daily. Doing this, you will have an opportunity to bond with your dog while giving him a thorough health inspection. Make it a fun time for both of you. Your dog will come away looking and feeling his best and you will have the satisfaction of knowing you are taking the best possible care of him.

The JRT is a double-coated breed that is seen in three varieties.

The smooth should have a dense undercoat with a harsh overcoat that will protect him from the elements and underbrush. The rough-coated JRT should have a very dense undercoat with an extremely coarse overcoat to protect him from the elements. The broken coat has elements of the rough and smooth.

Smooth coats shed more freely than the rough or broken coats, but all coat types shed continuously. Finding white hairs, year-round, on your clothing and furniture, is unavoidable with a Jack Russell in your household.

SUPPLIES

Items that you will need to groom your terrier are:

- rubber hound glove
- trimmer knife
- horsehair glove
- greyhound comb
- flea comb
- nail trimmer
- grooming stone
- finger toothbrush and paste
- straight shears
- styptic powder

To begin the care of your dog, place him on a table of a height that will make the dog accessible to work with and that is comfortable for your back.

GROOMING YOUR SMOOTH-COATED JACK RUSSELL

For a smooth-coated terrier, start with a thorough, all-over brushing, followed by a rubdown with a well soaked, tightly squeezed magnet cloth. This removes old hair and debris, giving a nice, fresh look to the coat. Then look the dog over for anything that may need attention: teeth, eyes, nails, injury to foot pads, fleas and ticks, an unusual smell in

Jack Russell Terriers have one of three coat types: smooth, broken or rough.

47

A weekly brushing is essential for any Jack Russell, regardless of his coat type.

In between this weekly schedule, you will want to brush the dog almost daily because of the free-shedding tendency of the smooth coat.

GROOMING YOUR ROUGH- OR BROKEN-COATED JACK RUSSELL

Begin the grooming of a rough or broken by thoroughly combing and brushing the dog to loosen dead hair and dirt.

Put the dog up on the table and thoroughly comb and brush the dog to loosen dead hair and dirt. Then, with your rubber hound glove on one hand and your horsehair glove on the other, alternately stroke the dog with each hand for five minutes. This soon becomes a favored procedure for the terrier and, again, gives you an opportunity to examine him.

Every week during the grooming session, "rake" the coat to remove excess undercoat. If this is not done, the top coat will begin to lift and start to look very untidy.

The coat of the Jack Russell is never sculpted, as it should not be altered in such a manner as to give it an artificial, overdone appearance.

the ears and so forth. (Any unusual smell or matter in the ears requires the attention of a veterinarian.)

Brushing your dog's teeth is not only possible, it helps to prevent tooth decay.

This is a natural earth dog and should reflect that attitude.

BATHING

Bathing a Jack Russell Terrier is not an event that is necessary in his life, unless he gets "skunked" or rolls in something completely objectionable or has a serious flea problem. If a bath truly becomes necessary, be sure the ears are plugged with cotton balls and the eyes are protected from soap.

The shampoo should be a harsh-coat preparation. Anything that contains a conditioner will prove detrimental to the jacket of the dog. Above all, be certain that all soapy residue is completely rinsed out and that the coat is thoroughly dried before the dog is returned to the outdoors. If you are bathing an aged animal, use a hair dryer to help dry the coat and keep the dog inside until he is completely dry, except for a brief time out to relieve himself.

NAILS

When clipping nails, work in the best possible light. You should be quite able to see the quick very clearly and not clip into it. (If a nail is black, cut it back about the same

49

distance as the clear ones, erring on the side of less distance than more.) Please do not try to cut as close as possible to the quick in the first few times you trim your dog's nails. And if you think a nail is not short enough after you have just cut it, do not repeat the clipping on that nail. Should you happen to nip the nail close enough to cause bleeding, quickly apply styptic powder. If you are in real doubt about foot care, it is best to have your veterinarian attend to it or assist you the first few times you do it—but do be sure that the nails are done. Nails that are too long can cause the dog to stand and move incorrectly and can harm the feet.

The most important thing to remember when you're clipping your JRT's nails is not to cut too much and nick the quick.

CHAPTER SIX

Measuring Up

The Jack Russell Terrier, also known as the Parson Jack Russell Terrier, is a small-in-size and big-in-attitude dog. This dog is highly intelligent and expressive, brave to the point of abandon and considered by some to be compulsive in behavior. They are also loving dogs with a great sense of humor that treasure their contact with humans. Although adaptable, this breed demands an enormous amount of physical and mental activity.

First and foremost, however, the Jack Russell is a hunting dog that works below ground. This terrier's structure is modeled after that of the vixen fox. Like the fox, the Jack Russell must be well angulated and possess a small, compressible chest that enables her to maneuver in small earthen tubes, often deep below ground. Interestingly, the Jack Russell is not considered to be a "pure" breed but is, rather, a strain or type of Fox Terrier. The Jack Russell Terrier has a broad standard and a broad genetic makeup, and does not necessarily breed true to type. This is the result of having been bred strictly for hunting since their beginnings in the early nineteenth century.

THE JACK RUSSELL TERRIER STANDARD

The Jack Russell Terrier Club of America, the oldest and largest JRT breed club and registry in the world, has adopted the standard set by the JRTC of Great Britain, guidelines

The overall impression of a Jack Russell Terrier should be one of a lively and fearless, yet cheerful, working dog.

51

designed to preserve and protect this working strain of terrier. Quotes from the standard appear in italics, followed by comments.

CHARACTERISTICS *The terrier must present a lively, active and alert appearance. It should impress with its fearless and happy disposition. It should be remembered that the Jack Russell is a working terrier and should retain these instincts. Nervousness, cowardice and over-aggressiveness should be discouraged, and it should always appear confident.*

The Jack Russell Terrier must be a lively, ready-for-action terrier, on her toes every waking moment.

A Jack Russell's head should carry a dark nose, well-formed muzzle and a lively, intelligent-looking pair of eyes.

JRTs have small V-shaped ears that fall forward on the head.

The Jack Russell breed standard allows the teeth to have a scissors bite or a level bite.

52

They are trigger-quick for action, and yet not nervous or yappy. They should not be cowardly, or demonstrate fearfulness by skulking or acting timid; the JRT is a hunting dog and has been bred for courage.

The Jack Russell should not be aggressive in her relations with humans. She has been bred as a hunting dog to hold her ground with quarry, but not to do battle.

GENERAL APPEARANCE *A sturdy, tough terrier, very much on its toes at all times, measuring between 10" and 15" at the withers. The body length must be in proportion to the height, and it should present a compact, balanced image, always being in solid, hard condition.*

The 5-inch variation between minimum and maximum heights may seem unusual, but the dogs produced under this broad standard provide their owners with the variety required to meet their needs. Different types of quarry require different-sized dogs.

HEAD *Should be well balanced and in proportion to the body. The skull should be flat, of moderate width at the ears, narrowing to the eyes. There should be a defined stop, but not* overpronounced. *The length of the muzzle from the nose to the stop should be slightly shorter than the distance from the stop to the occiput. The nose should be black. The jaw should be powerful and well-boned with strongly muscled cheeks.*

Unlike the Fox Terrier's head, the Jack Russell's head should have a defined, yet not too severe, stop. The head should be in harmony with the body. A tiny, weak-looking head is not appropriate for a hunting dog, nor is a massive head that looks as though it could stop up an earthen tunnel or make the dog appear head-heavy.

EYES *Should be almond-shaped, dark in color and full of life and intelligence.*

Unlike some other breeds, the Jack Russell Terrier likes to make and hold eye contact with people. In this gesture and in the alert, intelligent look in her eyes lie the expression of the true Jack Russell character: bold, fearless and eager.

EARS *Small V-shaped drop ears carried forward close to the head and of moderate thickness.*

The ears should not stand up (prick eared). Prick ears are a sign of past infusions of other breeds or are due to thick cartilage. Thick, houndish ears are likewise not desirable.

Because the JRT was bred to work in the field, not in the showring, scarred ears from encounters in the line of duty are not a defect. The terrier's ears fold over to help her in her job and are meant to protect the inner ear from dirt and other matter in the field.

MOUTH *Strong teeth with the top slightly overlapping the lower. Note: A level bite is acceptable for registration.*

The standard calls for a scissors bite, though it states clearly that a level bite is also acceptable.

NECK *Clean and muscular, of good length, gradually widening at the shoulders.*

FOREQUARTERS *Shoulders should be sloping and well laid back, fine at points and clearly cut at the withers. Forelegs should be strong and straight-boned with joints in correct alignment. Elbows hanging perpendicular to the body and working free of the sides.*

The laid-back angle of the shoulder blade specified in this part of the standard allows good movement at the front end of the dog.

53

A JRT's coat should be at least 51 percent white, with tan, black or brown markings.

BODY *The chest should be shallow, narrow and the front legs set not too widely apart, giving an athletic rather than a heavily chested appearance. As a guide only, the chest should be small enough to be easily spanned behind the shoulders, by average-sized hands, when the terrier is in fit, working condition. The back should be strong, straight and, in comparison to the height of the terrier, give a balanced image. The loin should be slightly arched.*

The chest size and shape are of utmost importance. A barrel- or keel-shaped chest would hinder the dog's ability to make her way through narrow passages below ground. A small, flexible chest that can be compressed in a tight place is vital, as a chesty dog cannot get far into an earthen tube.

HINDQUARTERS *Should be strong and muscular, well put together with*

good angulation and bend of stifle, giving plenty of drive and propulsion. Looking from behind, the hocks must be straight.

FEET *Round, hard-padded and of catlike appearance, turning neither in nor out.*

Compact, well-padded feet are very important to this working dog, as Jack Russells must be able to dig efficiently in various soil conditions. Dewclaws are removed so they don't catch and tear while the dog is working.

TAIL *Set rather high, carried gaily and in proportion to body length, usually about four inches long, providing a good hand-hold.*

The approximately 4-inch docked tail provides a good hand-hold for extracting the terrier from an earth tunnel when necessary. Undocked tails carry the risk of breaking while the dog backs up in tiny tunnels, and tails that are too short don't provide a good terrier-handle. One-third of a puppy's tail is docked when it is around 3 days old.

COAT *Smooth, without being so sparse as not to provide a certain* *amount of protection from the elements and undergrowth. Rough- or broken-coated, without being woolly.*

Since JRTs must spend hours below ground in dark, damp places, a good coat is necessary to provide protection. When traveling on the ground, a good coat protects the skin from thorns and helps to resist burdocks.

COLOR *White should predominate (i.e., more than 51 percent white) with tan, black or brown markings. Brindle markings are unacceptable.*

White has been favored partly because it was thought that hounds would be better able to distinguish the terrier from the fox, and partly so that a handler, after digging to the dog, would be able to immediately distinguish the quarry from the dog when both were covered with loose soil.

GAIT *Movement should be free, lively, well coordinated, with straight action in front and behind.*

SIZE *Please note: For showing purposes, terriers are classified into two groups: 10" to 12$\frac{1}{2}$" and over 12$\frac{1}{2}$" up to 15".*

Here is where there is room for variety for different purposes. Different types of quarry may require different sizes and working styles.

INJURIES *Old scars or injuries, the result of work or accident, should not be allowed to prejudice a terrier's chance*

WHAT IS A BREED STANDARD?

A breed standard—a detailed description of an individual breed—is meant to portray the ideal specimen of that breed. This includes ideal structure, temperament, gait, type—all aspects of the dog. Because the standard describes an ideal specimen, it isn't based on any particular dog. It is a concept against which judges compare actual dogs and breeders strive to produce dogs. At a dog show, the dog that wins is the one that comes closest, in the judge's opinion, to the standard for her breed. Breed standards are written by the breed parent clubs, the national organizations formed to oversee the well-being of the breed. The chest of the Jack Russell must be the correct size and shape for the dog to do the job she was bred for. White should be the dominant color in the Jack Russell's coat. The JRTCA does not register Jack Russells until they are a year old and conform to the high standards of health and soundness the club requires.

in the show ring unless they interfere with its movement or utility for work or stud.

Some working terriers may lose teeth while working, from biting and pulling through roots in their paths, and some are injured in encounters with an earth-dwelling resident. As long as the jaw is in correct alignment and its movement is not affected, such injuries are not counted against the terrier in the showring.

THE MALE *Male animals should have two apparently normal testicles fully descended into the scrotum.*

RELATION TO OTHER BREEDS
A Jack Russell Terrier should not show any strong characteristics of another breed.

Since the Jack Russell is a strain of Fox Terrier, influences from other breeds may sometimes surface in markings (such as brindle) or in soft or linty coat textures. The Jack Russell should no longer show any strong evidence of these old crosses.

FAULTS *Shyness. Disinterest. Overly aggressive. Defects in bite. Weak jaws. Fleshy ears. Down at shoulder. Barrel ribs. Out at the elbow.*

Narrow hips. Straight stifles. Weak feet. Sluggish or unsound movement. Dishing. Plaiting. Toeing. Silky or woolly coats. Too much color (less than 51 percent white). Shrill or weak voice. Lack of muscle or skin tone. Lack of stamina or lung reserve. Evidence of foreign blood.

The "Faults" section of the standard directly reflects the work the JRT was bred to do. The dog must be able to move well because her success below ground depends on her being able to do so. Defects of structure may hinder a dog and cause her demise if she is unable to work free from a small earthen tube. The terrier must speak below ground to mark the location of her quarry, so a good voice is desirable. A working terrier must be in prime condition, not unfit with soft muscles or loose skin. The terrier must be an athlete, up to the work required.

JACK RUSSELL TERRIER CLUBS

The Jack Russell Terrier Club of America, The Jack Russell Terrier Club of Great Britain and the majority of the rest of the Jack Russell clubs in the world, united

through the Jack Russell Terrier World Federation, had, until recently, strongly opposed recognition of this breed by any kennel club or national all-breed registry. On January 1, 1998 the Jack Russell Terrier joined the Miscellaneous Group of the American Kennel Club. JRTs will soon be transitioned into the Terrier Group. However, it remains of utmost importance to Jack Russell Terrier owners and working terrier people to preserve the working ability, high intelligence and sound physical structure of this terrier.

The Jack Russell Terrier Club of America

The Jack Russell Terrier Club of America (JRTCA), founded by Ailsa Crawford in 1976. It has been specifically designed to maintain the Jack Russell Terrier as a healthy working breed, as free as possible from genetic faults and characteristics that would be detrimental to the breed and its working heritage. The JRTCA considers an application for registration on the individual terrier's own merits—having registered parents does not automatically guarantee that the progeny can be registered.

JRTCA Standards of Excellence

A terrier is not eligible for registration with the JRTCA until she reaches 1 year of age and has attained adult height, dentition and other aspects of full maturity. The owner must be a current member in good standing with the JRTCA and every application for registration must be accompanied by the following documents:

- Veterinary Certificate
- Pedigree
- Stud Service Certificate
- Color Photographs

Working Qualifications

- Trial Certificate
- Sporting Certificate
- Natural Hunting Certificate
- JRTCA Bronze Medallion

For more information on the JRTCA standards and working qualifications, contact: The Jack Russell Terrier Club of America, P.O. Box 4527, Lutherville, MD 21094-4527.

STYLE AND PURPOSE

By tradition, the terrier is bred to be "soft." The dog is not to harm the animal she meets in its lair below ground, but she must have the courage to bolt it, forcing the quarry to leave its den through a tunnel and out an exit simply as a result of the brave little dog's presence. If the quarry will not or cannot bolt, the terrier should have the heart to stay with it while the owner digs down to the dog and her prize.

What, then, is the Jack Russell Terrier? She is, simply, an extension of the early unspoiled-by-showring-fashions strain of working Fox Terrier. It is vital to the future of this breed that potential owners know that the breed is, first and foremost, a hunting dog that has been kept sound through years of breeding strictly for working ability, temperament and intelligence. She is a little dog with a big heart that is happiest doing what she is bred to do: working hard to please her owner, and herself, in the field.

CHAPTER SEVEN

A Matter of Fact

ANCESTRY

The Reverend John Russell (1795–1883) of Devonshire, in the western part of England, developed one the world's finest strains of working terriers. These terriers were bred to work. Jack Russell was a colorful and flamboyant character, and he and his strain of terriers soon became well known.

The Fox Terrier

The original strains of Fox Terriers were based on what were called White Terriers, which now are

The Jack Russell breed originated from a long line of working dogs.

corners to catch up with the hounds, or even anticipate where the chase might end, to do his job right.

THE FOX TERRIER IN THE SHOWRING

The popularity of the terriers reached its zenith in the late nineteenth century, and Fox Terriers were accepted as an English Kennel Club breed. It was not long before the Fox Terrier was caught up in the whims of the showring.

The breed developed an upright scapula (shoulder blade), a deepened chest and a lengthened, narrowed head. In the showring a smooth coat was favored over the less popular but more protective wiry-haired coat (rough or broken coat). The showring's Fox Terrier was no longer at all like the working terriers in the hunt kennels. With their redesigned structure, they could not enter shallow earth even if the instinct to do so remained.

The Working Terrier

As the popular Fox Terrier went to the shows, John Russell and other working terrier men went into the fields and followed hounds in pursuit of quarry. Many a man lacking

extinct. Many British hunt kennels kept their own strains of terriers that worked with their hounds. The hounds would follow the fox in chase and put him to ground. The hounds and the field of riders following them would be moved back, and a terrier man or hunt staff member would enter a terrier after the fox. Quite often, just the presence of the baying little dog would suggest to the fox that he might wish to go elsewhere for refuge— and the chase would continue. Since the terrier ran with hounds and put in a hard day's work, good stamina and tenacity were required. Often he had to know how to cut wealth or a fine horse would keep a few terriers. The ability of a good working dog to afford a man some sport locating fox or badger meant more than any pedigree. With the limited transportation available in those days, the terriers were rather closely bred. Definite types began to develop region by region, with size and temperament suitable to the area. All of these types were called "hunt" or "fox" terriers.

The Reverend Jack Russell

John Russell's dogs were of a type suitable to the terrain of the west country where they lived. But, with the fame of both Reverend Russell and his dogs spreading, it became

WHERE DID DOGS COME FROM?

It can be argued that dogs were right there at man's side from the beginning of time. As soon as human beings began to document their own existence, the dog was among their drawings and inscriptions. Dogs were not just friends, they served a purpose: There were dogs to hunt birds, pull sleds, herd sheep, burrow after rats—even sit in laps! What your dog was originally bred to do influences the way he behaves.

61

the desirable thing in other parts of the country to have one of his terriers. Apart from his church activities, the reverend was well known throughout England as a man passionate for the sport of fox hunting

Like all terriers, the Jack Russell was bred to have stamina, an eagerness to please and an instinct to dig in search of quarry.

of courage, endurance and hardi-hood."

It has been reported that John Russell was not interested in the killing of the fox. He said of the terriers: "A real Fox Terrier is not meant to murder and his intelligence should always keep him from such a crime." When fair terrier work is possible, with a noncombative terrier employed, one can well understand John Russell's fondness for the chase alone.

Jack Russell himself is said to have been concerned that Jack Russell Terriers be bred to love the sport of hunting, but not of killing; he wanted them to be able to recognize the "play" involved.

and breeding fox-hunting dogs. It was not long before the name Jack Russell Terrier spread and began to develop as the permanent name of these feisty little working terriers.

The reverend's foundation bitch was named Trump. In Russell's eyes, Trump was the ideal terrier. She was white with brown ears, a patch of brown over each eye and one no larger than a British penny at the base of her tail. Her coat was reported to be thick, close and wiry, but not the long jacket of the Scottish terrier. Her legs were as straight as arrows, her feet were perfect and she was of a size that has been compared to a female fox. Said Russell of this lovely animal: "Her whole appearance gave indications

After Jack Russell

Jack Russell left a legacy of the hardy, old-fashioned, willing-to-work terrier. Those who did not hunt were culled along the way, or kept as pets in homes of non-sporting people. Others that did not conform correctly for earth work were kept by people who found they were useful above ground for the task of rodent control.

Fortunately, while the showring Fox Terrier continued to develop—and change—devoted fans of the original Fox Terrier continued to happily breed and work their dogs in both England and North America. During this time they were still called by many names:

hunt terrier, white terrier (after their extinct ancestor) and working Fox Terrier. Eventually, of course, the problem was settled. With the name Fox Terrier being so firmly, and publicly, connected to the show dog, the name Jack Russell Terrier became attached to the original strain of working terriers.

THE JACK RUSSELL TERRIER TODAY

The Jack Russell Terrier Club of America was founded in 1976. There are now, thousands of members dedicated to the protection of the Jack Russell Terrier.

The Jack Russell Terrier today is the unspoiled working terrier of the 1800s. The breed has been preserved by the working-related standards of most of the major terrier clubs. The mental and physical soundness of the Jack Russell Terrier is protected by those dedicated to their breed's work, performance and character.

Today, the Jack Russell is a much-loved pet in homes and families across the country. In addition to preserving the working function of the Jack Russell Terrier, the JRTCA serves to educate pet owners about the unique qualities and requirements of keeping a Jack Russell. The JRTCA offers

Advocates for the purity of the Jack Russell breed contend that breeders must work to maintain the dog's true terrier instincts, not alter them to make the breed more suitable for the dog show stage.

The Jack Russell Terrier is fearless enough to be comfortable around large animals like horses.

services and activities to keep people working and bonding with these special dogs. The club encourages people to love, play with and work their terriers, and to fight for the dogs' ability to work, both now and in the future.

The Jack Russell as a Pet

Jack Russell Terriers these days continue as adaptable and amusing companions. Still comfortable around stables, they have no fear of the large horses in their lives. They may do well with some other breeds of dogs, but not all, much preferring the company of their own. Even then, care must be exercised. They are quite sensitive and, if harshly punished, slow to forgive—if they forgive at all.

A properly trained Jack Russell Terrier is a perfect pet for any environment. However, the stresses of confinement in cramped areas with limited outlets for their natural curiosity, and the sometimes compulsive behavior of an unemployed working dog, create a recipe for destruction. JRT owners need to understand the unique personality of this breed to keep them well-adjusted in the home.

FAMOUS OWNERS OF JACK RUSSELL TERRIERS

Bette Midler	Prince Charles
Mariah Carey	Ian Dunbar
Audrey Hepburn	James Herriot
Andrew Wyeth	

CHAPTER EIGHT

On Good Behavior

by Ian Dunbar, Ph.D., MRCVS

Training is the jewel in the crown—the most important aspect of doggy husbandry. There is no more important variable influencing dog behavior and temperament than the dog's education: A well-trained, well-behaved and good-natured puppydog is always a joy to live with, but an untrained and uncivilized dog can be a perpetual nightmare. Moreover, deny the dog an education and she will not have the opportunity to fulfill her own canine potential; neither will she have the ability to communicate effectively with her human companions.

Luckily, modern psychological training methods are easy, efficient, effective and, above all, considerably dog-friendly and user-friendly. Doggy education is as simple as it is enjoyable. But before you can have a good time play-training with your new dog, you have to learn what to do and how to do it. There is no bigger variable influencing the success of dog training than the

When your puppy gets into something he shouldn't, take it away and show him the proper alternative.

owner's experience and expertise. Before you embark on the dog's education, you must first educate yourself.

BASIC TRAINING FOR OWNERS

Ideally, basic owner training should begin well before you select your dog. Find out all you can about your chosen breed first, then master rudimentary training and handling skills. If you already have your puppydog, owner training is a dire emergency—the clock is ticking! Especially for puppies, the first few weeks at home are the most important and influential days in the dog's life. Indeed, the cause of most adolescent and adult problems may be traced back to the initial days the pup explores her new home. This is the time to establish the *status quo*—to teach the puppydog how you would like her to behave and so prevent otherwise quite predictable problems.

In addition to consulting breeders and breed books such as this one (which understandably have a positive breed bias), seek out as many pet owners with your breed as you can find. Good points are obvious. What you want to find out are the breed-specific problems, so you can nip them in the bud. In particular, you should talk to owners with adolescent dogs and make a list of all anticipated problems. Most important, test drive at least half a dozen adolescent and adult dogs of your breed yourself. An 8-week-old puppy is deceptively easy to handle, but she will acquire adult size, speed and strength in just four months, so you should learn now what to prepare for.

Puppy and pet dog training classes offer a convenient venue to locate pet owners and observe dogs in action. For a list of suitable trainers in your area, contact the Association of Pet Dog Trainers at 800-PET-DOGS.

PRINCIPLES OF TRAINING

Most people think training comprises teaching the dog to do things such as sit, speak and roll over, but even a 4-week-old pup knows how to do these things already. Instead, the first step in training involves teaching the dog human words for each dog behavior and activity and for each aspect of the dog's environment. That way you, the owner, can more easily participate in the dog's domestic education by directing her to perform specific actions appropriately, that is, at the right time, in the right place and so on. Training opens communication channels, enabling an educated dog to at least understand her owner's requests.

In addition to teaching a dog what we want her to do, it is also necessary to teach her why she should do what we ask. Indeed, 95 percent of training revolves around motivating the dog to want to do what we want. Dogs often understand what their owners want; they just don't see the point of doing it—especially when the owner's repetitively boring and seemingly senseless instructions are totally at odds with much more pressing and exciting doggy distractions. It is not so much the dog that is being stubborn or dominant; rather, it is the owner who has failed to acknowledge the dog's needs and feelings and to approach training from the dog's point of view.

The Meaning of Instructions

The secret to successful training is learning how to use training lures to predict or prompt specific behaviors—to coax the dog to do what you want when you want.

Any highly valued object (such as a treat or toy) may be used as a lure, which the dog will follow with her eyes and nose. Moving the lure in specific ways entices the dog to move her nose, head and entire body in specific ways. In fact, by learning the art of manipulating various lures, it is possible to teach the dog to assume virtually any body position and perform any action. Once you have control over the expression of the dog's behaviors and can elicit any body position or behavior at will, you can easily teach the dog to perform on request.

Tell your dog what you want her to do, use a lure to entice her to respond correctly, then profusely praise and maybe reward her once she performs the desired action. For example, verbally request "Fido, sit!" while you move a squeaky toy upwards and backwards over the dog's muzzle (lure-movement and hand signal), smile knowingly as she looks up (to follow the lure) and sits down (as a result of canine anatomical engineering), then praise her to distraction ("Gooood Fido!"). Squeak the toy, offer a training treat and give your dog and yourself a pat on the back.

Being able to elicit desired responses over and over enables the owner to reward the dog over and over. Consequently, the dog begins to think training is fun. For example, the more the dog is rewarded for sitting, the more she enjoys sitting. Eventually the dog comes to realize that, whereas most sitting is appreciated, sitting immediately upon request usually prompts especially enthusiastic praise and a slew of high-level rewards. The dog begins to sit on cue much of the time, showing that she is starting to grasp the meaning of the owner's verbal request and hand signal.

Why Comply?

Most dogs enjoy initial lure-reward training and are only too happy to comply with their owners' wishes. Unfortunately, repetitive drilling without appreciative feedback tends to diminish the dog's enthusiasm until she eventually fails to see the point of complying anymore. Moreover, as the dog approaches adolescence she becomes more easily distracted as she develops other interests. Lengthy sessions with repetitive exercises tend to bore and demotivate both parties. If it's not fun, the owner doesn't do it and neither does the dog. Integrate training into your dog's life: The greater number of training sessions each day and the shorter they are, the more willingly compliant your dog will become.

Punishment

Without a doubt, lure-reward training is by far the best way to teach: Entice your dog to do what you want and then reward her for doing so. Unfortunately, a human shortcoming is to take the good for granted and to moan and groan at the bad. Specifically, the dog's many good behaviors are ignored while the owner focuses on punishing the dog for making mistakes. In extreme cases, instruction is limited to punishing mistakes made by a trainee dog, child, employee or husband, even though it has been proven punishment training is notoriously inefficient and ineffective and is decidedly unfriendly and combative. It teaches the dog that training is a drag, almost as quickly as it teaches the dog to dislike her

trainer. Why treat our best friends like our worst enemies?

Punishment training is also much more laborious and time-consuming. Whereas it takes only a finite amount of time to teach a dog what to chew, for example, it takes much, much longer to punish the dog for each and every mistake. Remember, there is only one right way! So why not teach that right way from the outset?!

To make matters worse, punishment training causes severe lapses in the dog's reliability. Since it is obviously impossible to punish the dog each and every time she misbehaves, the dog quickly learns to distinguish between those times when she must comply (so as to avoid impending punishment) and those times when she need not comply, because punishment is impossible. Such times include when the dog is off leash and 6 feet away, when the owner is otherwise engaged (talking to a friend, watching television, taking a shower, tending to the baby or chatting on the telephone) or when the dog is left at home alone.

Instances of misbehavior will be numerous when the owner is away, because even when the dog complied in the owner's looming presence, she did so unwillingly. The dog was forced to act against her will, rather than molding her will to want to please. Hence, when the owner is absent, not only does the dog know she need not comply, she simply does not want to. Again, the trainee is not a stubborn vindictive beast, but rather the trainer has failed to teach. Punishment training invariably creates unpredictable Jekyll and Hyde behavior.

TRAINER'S TOOLS

Many training books extol the virtues of a vast array of training paraphernalia. In reality, most effective training tools are not found in stores; they come from within ourselves. In addition to a willing dog,

all you really need is a functional human brain, gentle hands, a loving heart and a good attitude.

In terms of equipment, all dogs do require a quality buckle collar to sport dog tags and to attach the leash (for safety and to comply with local leash laws). Hollow chew toys (like Kongs or sterilized longbones) and a dog bed or collapsible crate are musts for housetraining. Three additional tools are required:

1. specific lures (training treats and toys) to predict and prompt specific desired behaviors;

2. rewards (praise, affection, training treats and toys) to reinforce for the dog what a lot of fun it all is; and

3. knowledge—how to convert the dog's favorite activities and

You always have to have your eyes open and your thinking cap on when there are Jack Russell puppies around.

games (potential distractions to training) into "life-rewards," which may be employed to facilitate training.

The most powerful of these is knowledge. Education is the key!

HOUSETRAINING

If dogs were left to their own devices, certainly they would chew, dig and bark for entertainment and then no doubt highlight a few areas of their living space with sprinkles of urine, in much the same way we decorate by hanging pictures. Consequently, when we ask a dog to live with us, we must teach her *where* she may dig, *where* she may perform her toilet duties, *what* she may chew and *when* she may bark. After all, when left at home alone for many hours, we cannot expect the dog to amuse herself by completing crosswords or watching the soaps on TV!

Also, it would be decidedly unfair to keep the house rules a secret from the dog, and then get angry and punish the poor critter for inevitably transgressing rules she did not even know existed. Remember:

Without adequate education and guidance, the dog will be forced to establish her own rules—doggy rules—and most probably will be at odds with the owner's view of domestic living.

Since most problems develop during the first few days the dog is at home, prospective dog owners must be certain they are quite clear about the principles of housetraining *before* they get a dog. Early misbehaviors quickly become established as the *status quo*—becoming firmly entrenched as hard-to-break bad habits, which set the precedent for years to come. Make sure to teach your dog good habits right from the start. Good habits are just as hard to break as bad ones!

Ideally, when a new dog comes home, try to arrange for someone to be present as much as possible during the first few days (for adult dogs) or weeks for puppies. With only a little forethought, it is surprisingly easy to find a puppy sitter, such as a retired person, who would be willing to eat from your refrigerator and watch your television while keeping an eye on the newcomer to encourage the dog to play with chew toys and to ensure she goes outside on a regular basis.

Potty Training

To teach the dog where to relieve herself:

1. never let her make a single mistake;

2. let her know where you want her to go; and

3. handsomely reward her for doing so: "GOOOOOOOD DOG!!!" liver treat, liver treat, liver treat!

Preventing Mistakes

A single mistake is a training disaster, since it heralds many more in future weeks. And each time the dog soils the house, this further reinforces the dog's unfortunate preference for an indoor, carpeted toilet. Do not let an unhouse-trained dog have full run of the house.

When you are away from home, or cannot pay full attention, confine the dog to an area where elimination is appropriate, such as an outdoor run or, better still, a small, comfort-able indoor kennel with access to an outdoor run. When confined in this manner, most dogs will naturally housetrain themselves.

If that's not possible, confine the dog to an area, such as a utility room, kitchen, basement or garage, where elimination may not be desired in the long run but as an interim measure it is certainly preferable to doing it all around the house. Use newspaper to cover the floor of the dog's day room. The newspaper may be used to soak up the urine and to wrap up and dis-pose of the feces. Once your dog develops a preferred spot for elimi-nating, it is only necessary to cover that part of the floor with news-paper. The smaller papered area may then be moved (only a little each day) towards the door to the outside. Thus the dog will develop the tendency to go to the door when she needs to relieve herself.

Never confine an unhousetrained dog to a crate for long periods. Do-ing so would force the dog to soil the crate and ruin its usefulness as an aid for housetraining (see the fol-lowing discussion).

Teaching Where

In order to teach your dog where you would like her to do her busi-ness, you have to be there to direct the proceedings—an obvious, yet often neglected, fact of life. In order to be there to teach the dog where to go, you need to know *when* she needs to go. Indeed, the success of housetraining depends on the owner's ability to predict these times. Certainly, a regular feeding schedule will facilitate prediction somewhat, but there is nothing like "loading the deck" and influencing the timing of the outcome yourself!

Whenever you are at home, make sure the dog is under constant supervision and/or confined to a small area. If already well trained, simply instruct the dog to lie down in her bed or basket. Alternatively, confine the dog to a crate (doggy den) or tie-down (a short, 18-inch lead that can be clipped to an eye hook in the baseboard near her bed). Short-term close confinement strongly inhibits urination and defecation, since the dog does not want to soil her sleeping area. Thus, when you release the puppydog each hour, she will definitely need to urinate immediately and defecate every third or fourth hour. Keep the dog confined to her doggy den and take her to her intended toilet area each hour, every hour on the hour. When taking your dog outside, instruct her to sit quietly before opening the

door—she will soon learn to sit by the door when she needs to go out!

Teaching Why

Being able to predict when the dog needs to go enables the owner to be on the spot to praise and reward the dog. Each hour, hurry the dog to the intended toilet area in the yard, issue the appropriate instruction ("Go pee!" or "Go poop!"), then give the dog three to four minutes to produce. Praise and offer a couple of training treats when successful. The treats are important because many people fail to praise their dogs with feeling . . . and housetraining is hardly the time for understatement. So either loosen up and enthusiastically praise that dog: "Wuzzzer-wuzzer-wuzzer, hoooser good wuffer den? Hoooo went pee for Daddy?" Or say "Good dog!" as best you can and offer the treats for effect.

Following elimination is an ideal time for a spot of play-training in the yard or house. Also, an empty dog may be allowed greater freedom around the house for the next half hour or so, just as long as you keep an eye out to make sure she does not get into other kinds of mischief. If you are preoccupied and cannot pay full attention, confine the dog to her doggy den once more to enjoy a peaceful snooze or to play with her many chew toys.

If your dog does not eliminate within the allotted time outside—no biggie! Back to her doggy den, and then try again after another hour.

Beware of falling into the trap of walking the dog to get her to eliminate. The good ol' dog walk is such an enormous highlight in the dog's life that it represents the single biggest potential reward in domestic dogdom. However, when in a hurry, or during inclement weather, many owners abruptly terminate the walk the moment the dog has done her business. This, in effect, severely punishes the dog for doing the right thing, in the right place at the right time. Consequently, many dogs become strongly inhibited from eliminating outdoors because they know it will signal an abrupt end to an otherwise thoroughly enjoyable walk.

Instead, instruct the dog to relieve herself in the yard prior to going for a walk. You will find with a "No feces—no walk" policy, your dog will become one of the fastest defecators in the business.

If you do not have a backyard, instruct the dog to eliminate right outside your front door prior to the walk. Not only will this facilitate cleanup and disposal of the feces in your own trash can but, also, the walk may again be used as a colossal reward.

CHEWING AND BARKING

Short-term close confinement also teaches the dog that occasional quiet moments are a reality of domestic living. Your puppydog is extremely impressionable during her first few weeks at home. Regular confinement at this time soon exerts a calming influence over the dog's personality. Remember, once the dog is housetrained and calmer, there will be a whole lifetime ahead for the dog to enjoy full run of the house and garden. On the other hand, by letting the newcomer have unrestricted access to the entire household and allowing her to run willy-nilly, she will most certainly develop a bunch of behavior problems in short order, no doubt necessitating confinement later in life.

When confining the dog, make sure she always has an impressive array of suitable chew toys. Kongs and sterilized longbones (both

74

readily available from pet stores) make the best chew toys, since they are hollow and may be stuffed with treats to heighten the dog's interest.

Remember, treats do not have to be junk food and they certainly should not represent extra calories. Rather, treats should be part of each dog's regular daily diet: Some food may be served in the dog's bowl for breakfast and dinner, some food may be used as training treats, and some food may be used for stuffing chew toys. I regularly stuff my dogs' many Kongs with different shaped biscuits and kibble. The kibble seems to fall out fairly easily, as do the oval-shaped biscuits, thus rewarding the dog instantaneously for checking out the chew toys. The bone-shaped biscuits fall out after a while, rewarding the dog for worrying at the chew toy. But the triangular biscuits never come out. They remain inside the Kong as lures, maintaining the dog's fascination with her chew toy. To further focus the dog's interest, I always make sure to flavor the triangular biscuits by rubbing them with a little cheese or freeze-dried liver.

If stuffed chew toys are reserved especially for times the dog is confined, the puppydog will soon learn to enjoy quiet moments in her doggy den and she will quickly develop a chew-toy habit—a good habit! This is a simple autoshaping process; all the owner has to do is set up the situation and the dog all but trains herself—easy and effective. Even when the dog is given run of the house, her first inclination will be to indulge her rewarding chew-toy habit rather than destroy less attractive household articles, such as curtains, carpets, chairs and compact disks. Similarly, a chew-toy chewer will be less inclined to scratch and chew herself excessively. Also, if the dog busies herself as a recreational chewer, she will be less inclined to develop into a recreational barker or digger when left at home alone.

Stuff a number of chew toys whenever the dog is left confined and remove the extra-special-tasting treats when you return. Your dog will now amuse herself with her chew toys before falling asleep and then resume playing with her chew toys when she expects you to return. Since most owner-absent misbehavior happens right after you leave and right before your expected return, your puppydog will now be conveniently preoccupied with her chew toys at these times.

COME AND SIT

Most puppies will happily approach virtually anyone, whether called or not; that is, until they collide with adolescence and develop other more important doggy interests, such as sniffing a multiplicity of exquisite odors on the grass. Your mission, Mr./Ms. Owner, is to teach and reward the pup for coming reliably, willingly and happily when called—and you have just three months to get it done. Unless adequately reinforced, your puppy's tendency to approach people will self-destruct by adolescence.

Call your dog ("Fido, come!"), open your arms (and maybe squat down) as a welcoming signal, waggle a treat or toy as a lure and reward the puppydog when she comes running. Do not wait to praise the dog until she reaches you—she may come 95 percent of the way and then run off after some distraction. Instead, praise the dog's first step toward you and continue praising enthusiastically for every step she takes in your direction.

When the rapidly approaching puppydog is three lengths away from impact, instruct her to sit ("Fido, sit!") and hold the lure in front of

you in an outstretched hand to prevent her from hitting you midchest and knocking you flat on your back! As Fido decelerates to nose the lure, move the treat upwards and backwards just over her muzzle with an upwards motion of your extended arm (palm-upwards). As the dog looks up to follow the lure, she will sit down (if she jumps up, you are holding the lure too high). Praise the dog for sitting. Move backwards and call her again. Repeat this many times over, always praising when Fido comes and sits; on occasion, reward her.

For the first couple of trials, use a training treat both as a lure to entice the dog to come and sit and as a reward for doing so. Thereafter, try to use different items as lures and rewards. After just a few repetitions, dispense with the lures and rewards; the dog will begin to respond willingly to your verbal requests and hand signals just for the prospect of praise from your heart and affection from your hands.

Instruct every family member, friend and visitor how to get the dog to come and sit. Unless you teach your dog how to meet people, that is, to sit for greetings, no doubt the dog will resort to jumping up.

To teach come, call your dog, open your arms as a welcoming signal, wave a toy or a treat and praise for every step in your direction.

Then you and the visitors will get annoyed, and the dog will be punished. This is not fair.

Even though your dog quickly masters obedient recalls in the house, her reliability may falter when playing in the backyard or local park. Ironically, it is the owner who has unintentionally trained the dog not to respond in these instances. By allowing the dog to play and run around and otherwise have a good time, but then to call the dog to put her on leash to take her home, the dog quickly learns playing is fun but training is a drag. Thus, playing in the park becomes a severe distraction, which works against training. Bad news!

Instead, whether playing with the dog off leash or on leash, request her to come at frequent intervals—say, every minute or so. On most occasions, praise and pet the dog for a few seconds while she is sitting, then tell her to go play again. For especially fast recalls, offer a couple of training treats and take the time to praise and pet the dog enthusiastically before releasing her. The dog will learn that coming when called is not necessarily the end of the play session, and neither is it the end of the world; rather, it signals an enjoyable, quality time-out with the owner before resuming play once more. In fact, playing in the park now becomes a very effective life-reward, which works to facilitate training by reinforcing each obedient and timely recall. Good news!

SIT, DOWN, STAND AND ROLLOVER

Teaching the dog a variety of body positions is easy for owner and dog, impressive for spectators and extremely useful for all. Using lure-reward techniques, it is possible to train several positions at once to verbal commands or hand signals (which impress the socks off of onlookers).

Sit and down—the two control commands—prevent or resolve nearly a hundred behavior problems. For example, if the dog happily and obediently sits or lies down when requested, she cannot jump on visitors, dash out the front door, run around and chase her tail, pester other dogs, harass cats or annoy family, friends or strangers. Additionally, "Sit" or "Down" are the best emergency commands for off-leash control.

It is easier to teach and maintain a reliable sit than maintain a reliable recall. Sit is the purest and simplest of commands—either the dog is sitting or she is not. If there is any change of circumstances or potential danger in the park, for example, simply instruct the dog to sit. If she sits, you have a number of options:

Allow the dog to resume playing when she is safe, walk up and put the dog on leash or call the dog. The dog will be much more likely to come when called if she has already acknowledged her compliance by sitting. If the dog does not sit in the park—train her to!

Stand and rollover-stay are the two positions for examining the dog. Your veterinarian will love you to distraction if you take a little time to teach the dog to stand still and roll over and play possum.

As with teaching come and sit, the training techniques to teach the dog to assume all other body positions on cue are user-friendly and dog-friendly. Simply give the appropriate request, lure the dog into the desired body position using a training treat or toy and then praise (and maybe reward) the dog as soon as she complies. Try not to touch the dog to get her to respond. If you teach the dog by guiding her into position, the dog will quickly learn that rump-pressure means sit, for example, but as yet you still have no control over your dog if she is just 6 feet away. It will still be necessary to teach the dog to sit on request. So do not make training a time-consuming, two-step process;

instead, teach the dog to sit to a verbal request or hand signal from the outset. Once the dog sits willingly when requested, by all means use your hands to pet the dog when she does so.

To teach down when the dog is already sitting, say "Fido, down!," hold the lure in one hand (palm down) and lower that hand to the floor between the dog's forepaws. As the dog lowers her head to follow the lure, slowly move the lure away from the dog just a fraction (in front of her paws). The dog will lie down as she stretches her nose forward to follow the lure. Praise the dog when she does so. If the dog stands up, you pulled the lure away too far and too quickly.

When teaching the dog to lie down from the standing position, say "Down" and lower the lure to the floor as before. Once the dog has lowered her forequarters and assumed a play bow, gently and slowly move the lure towards the dog between her forelegs. Praise the dog as soon as her rear end plops down.

You will notice the more energetically you move your arm—upwards (palm up) to get the dog to sit, and downwards (palm down)

to get the dog to lie down—the more energetically the dog responds to your requests. Now try training the dog in silence and you will notice she has also learned to respond to hand signals. Yeah! Not too shabby for the first session.

To teach stand from the sitting position, say "Fido, stand," slowly move the lure half a dog-length away from the dog's nose, keeping it at nose level, and praise the dog as she stands to follow the lure. As soon as the dog stands, lower the lure to just beneath the dog's chin to entice her to look down; otherwise she will stand and then sit immediately. To prompt the dog to stand from the down position, move the lure half a dog-length upwards and

Puppies have short attention spans, so keep your training sessions short at first.

Using a food lure to teach sit, down and stand.
1) "Phoenix, sit."
2) Hand palm upwards, move lure up and back over dog's muzzle.
3) "Good sit, Phoenix!"

4) "Phoenix, down."
5) Hand palm downwards, move lure down to lie between dog's forepaws.
6) "Phoenix, off. Good down, Phoenix!"

7) "Phoenix, sit!"
8) Palm upwards, move lure up and back, keeping it close to dog's muzzle.
9) "Good sit, Phoenix!"

10) "Phoenix, stand!"
11) Move lure away from dog at nose height, then lower it a tad.
12) "Phoenix, off! Good stand, Phoenix!"

81

13) "Phoenix, down!"
14) Hand palm downwards, move lure down to lie between dog's forepaws.
15) "Phoenix, off! Good down-stay, Phoenix!"

16) "Phoenix, stand!"
17) Move lure away from dog's muzzle up to nose height.
18) "Phoenix, off! Good stand-stay, Phoenix. Now we'll make the vet and groomer happy!"

away from the dog, holding the lure at standing nose height from the floor.

Teaching rollover is best started from the down position, with the dog lying on one side, or at least with both hind legs stretched out on the same side. Say "Fido, bang!" and move the lure backwards and alongside the dog's muzzle to her elbow (on the side of her outstretched hind legs). Once the dog looks to the side and backwards, very slowly move the lure upwards to the dog's shoulder and backbone. Tickling the dog in the goolies (groin area) often invokes a reflex-raising of the hind leg as an appeasement gesture, which facilitates the tendency to roll over. If you move the lure too quickly and the dog jumps into the standing position, have patience and start again. As soon as the dog rolls onto her back, keep the lure stationary and mesmerize the dog with a relaxing tummy rub.

To teach rollover-stay when the dog is standing or moving, say "Fido, bang!" and give the appropriate hand signal (with index finger pointed and thumb cocked in true Sam Spade fashion), then in one fluid movement lure her to first lie down and then rollover-stay as above.

Teaching the dog to stay in each of the above four positions becomes a piece of cake after first teaching the dog not to worry at the toy or treat training lure. This is best accomplished by hand feeding dinner kibble. Hold a piece of kibble firmly in your hand and softly instruct "Off!" Ignore any licking and slobbering for however long the dog worries at the treat, but say "Take it!" and offer the kibble *the instant* the dog breaks contact with her muzzle. Repeat this a few times, and then up the ante and insist the dog remove her muzzle for one whole second before offering the kibble. Then progressively refine your criteria and have the dog not touch your hand (or treat) for longer and longer periods on each trial, such as for two seconds, four seconds, then six, ten, fifteen, twenty, thirty seconds and so on.

The dog soon learns: (1) worrying at the treat never gets results, whereas (2) noncontact is often rewarded after a variable time lapse.

Teaching "Off!" has many useful applications in its own right. Additionally, instructing the dog not to touch a training lure often produces spontaneous and magical stays. Request the dog to stand-stay, for example, and not to touch the lure. At first set your sights on a short two-second stay before rewarding the dog. (Remember, every long journey begins with a single step.) However, on subsequent trials, gradually and progressively increase the length of stay required to receive a reward. In no time at all your dog will stand calmly for a minute or so.

RELEVANCY TRAINING

Once you have taught the dog what you expect her to do when requested to come, sit, lie down, stand, roll over and stay, the time is right to teach the dog why she should comply with your wishes. The secret is to have many (many) extremely short training interludes (two to five seconds each) at numerous times during the course of the dog's day.

In no time at all the dog will be only too pleased to follow your instructions because she has learned that a compliant response heralds all sorts of goodies. Basically all you are trying to teach the dog is how to say please: "Please throw the tennis ball."

In fact, the dog may be unable to distinguish between training

and good times and, indeed, there should be no distinction. The warped concept that training involves forcing the dog to comply and/or dominating her will is totally at odds with the picture of a truly well-trained dog. In reality, enjoying a game of training with a dog is no different from enjoying a game of backgammon or tennis with a friend; and walking with a dog should be no different from strolling with a spouse, or with buddies on the golf course.

WALK BY YOUR SIDE

Many people attempt to teach a dog to heel by putting her on a leash and physically correcting the dog when she makes mistakes. There are a number of things seriously wrong with this approach, the first being that most people do not want precision heeling; rather, they simply want the dog to follow or walk by their side. Second, when physically restrained during "training," even though the dog may grudgingly mope by your side when "handcuffed" on leash, let's see what happens when she is off leash. History! The dog is in the next county because she never enjoyed walking with you on leash and you have no control over her off leash. So let's just teach the dog off leash from the outset to want to walk with us. Third, if the dog has not been trained to heel, it is a trifle hasty to think about punishing the poor dog for making mistakes and breaking heeling rules she didn't even know existed. This is simply not fair! Surely, if the dog had been adequately taught how to heel, she would seldom make mistakes and hence there would be no need to correct the dog. Remember, each mistake and each correction (punishment) advertise the trainer's

inadequacy, not the dog's. The dog is not stubborn, she is not stupid and she is not bad. Even if she were, she would still require training, so let's train her properly.

Let's teach the dog to enjoy following us and to want to walk by our side off leash. Then it will be easier to teach high-precision off-leash heeling patterns if desired. Before going on outdoor walks, it is necessary to teach the dog not to pull. Then it becomes easy to teach on-leash walking and heeling because the dog already wants to walk with you, she is familiar with the desired walking and heeling positions and she knows not to pull.

To get your puppy used to wearing a leash, have him take a trip or two around the house on lead.

FOLLOWING

Start by training your dog to follow you. Many puppies will follow if you simply walk away from them and maybe click your fingers or chuckle. Adult dogs may require additional enticement to stimulate them to follow, such as a training lure or, at the very least, a lively trainer. To teach the dog to follow: (1) keep walking and (2) walk away from the dog. If the dog attempts to lead or lag, change pace; slow down if the dog forges too far ahead, but speed up if she lags too far behind. Say "Steady!" or "Easy!" each time before you slow down and "Quickly!" or "Hustle!" each time before you speed up, and the dog will learn to change pace on cue. If the dog lags or leads too far, or if she wanders right or left, simply walk quickly in the opposite direction and maybe even run away from the dog and hide.

Practicing is a lot of fun; you can set up a course in your home, yard or park to do this. Indoors, entice the dog to follow upstairs, into a bedroom, into the bathroom, downstairs, around the living room couch, zigzagging between dining room chairs and into the kitchen for dinner. Outdoors, get the dog to follow around park benches, trees, shrubs and along walkways and lines in the grass. (For safety outdoors, it is advisable to attach a long line on the dog, but never exert corrective tension on the line.)

Remember, following has a lot to do with attitude—your attitude! Most probably your dog will not want to follow Mr. Grumpy Troll with the personality of wilted lettuce. Lighten up—walk with a jaunty step, whistle a happy tune, sing, skip and tell jokes to your dog, and she will be right by your side.

BY YOUR SIDE

It is smart to train the dog to walk close on one side or the other—either side will do, your choice. When walking, jogging or cycling, it is generally bad news to have the dog suddenly cut in front of you. In fact, I train my dogs to walk "By my side" and "Other side"—both very useful instructions. It is possible to position the dog fairly accurately by looking to the appropriate side and clicking your fingers or slapping your thigh on that side. A precise positioning may be attained by holding a training lure, such as a chew toy, tennis ball, or food treat. Stop and stand still several times throughout the walk, just as you would when window shopping or meeting a friend. Use the lure to make sure the dog slows down and stays close whenever you stop.

When teaching the dog to heel, we generally want her to sit in heel position when we stop. Teach heel position at the standstill and the dog will learn that the default heel position is sitting by your side (left or right—your choice, unless you wish to compete in obedience trials, in which case the dog must heel on the left).

Several times a day, stand up and call your dog to come and sit in heel position—"Fido, heel!" For example, instruct the dog to come to heel each time there are commercials on TV, or each time you turn a page of a novel, and the dog will get it in a single evening.

Practice straight-line heeling and turns separately. With the dog sitting at heel, teach her to turn in place. After each quarter-turn, half-turn or full turn in place, lure the dog to sit at heel. Now it's time for short straight-line heeling sequences, no more than a few steps at a time. Always think of heeling in terms of sit-heel-sit sequences—start and end with the dog in position and do your best to keep her there when moving. Progressively increase the number of steps in each sequence. When the dog remains close for 20 yards of straight-line heeling, it is time to add a few turns and then sign up for a happy-heeling obedience class to get some advice from the experts.

NO PULLING ON LEASH

You can start teaching your dog not to pull on leash anywhere—in front of the television or outdoors—but regardless of location, you must not take a single step with tension in the leash. For a reason known only to dogs, even just a couple of paces of pulling on leash is intrinsically motivating and diabolically rewarding. Instead, attach the leash to the dog's collar, grasp the other end firmly with both hands held close to your chest, and stand still—do not budge an inch. Have somebody watch you with a stopwatch to time your progress, or else you will never believe this will work and so you will not even try the exercise, and your shoulder and the dog's neck will be traumatized for years to come.

Stand still and wait for the dog to stop pulling, and to sit and/or lie down. All dogs stop pulling and sit eventually. Most take only a couple of minutes; the all-time record is $22\frac{1}{2}$ minutes. Time how long it takes. Gently praise the dog when she stops pulling, and as soon as she sits, enthusiastically praise the dog and take just one step forwards; then immediately stand still. This single step usually demonstrates the ballistic reinforcing nature of pulling on leash; most dogs explode to the end of the leash, so be prepared for the strain. Stand firm and wait for the dog to sit again. Repeat this half a dozen times and you will probably notice a progressive reduction in the force of the dog's one-step explosions and a radical reduction in the time it takes for the dog to sit each time.

As the dog learns "Sit we go" and "Pull we stop," she will begin to walk forward calmly with each single step and automatically sit when you stop. Now try two steps before you stop. Wooooooo! Scary! When the dog has mastered two steps at a time, try for three. After each success, progressively increase the number of steps in the sequence: Try four steps and then six, eight, ten and twenty steps before stopping. Congratulations! You are now walking the dog on leash.

Whenever walking with the dog (off leash or on leash), make sure you stop periodically to practice a few position commands and stays before instructing the dog to "Walk on!" (Remember, you want the dog to be compliant everywhere, not just in the kitchen when her dinner is at hand.) For example, stopping every 25 yards to briefly train the dog amounts to over 200 training interludes within a single 3-mile stroll. And each training session is

in a different location. You will not believe the improvement within just the first mile of the first walk.

To put it another way, integrating training into a walk offers 200 separate opportunities to use the continuance of the walk as a reward to reinforce the dog's education. Moreover, some training interludes may comprise continuing education for the dog's walking skills: Alternate short periods of the dog walking calmly by your side with periods when the dog is allowed to sniff and investigate the environment. Now sniffing odors on the grass and meeting other dogs become rewards which reinforce the dog's calm and mannerly demeanor.

Jack Russells are more than happy to perform jumping tricks for you, even without training.

CHAPTER NINE

Further Reading and Resources

BOOKS

About Jack Russell Terriers

Atter, Sheila. *The Jack Russell Terrier Today.* New York: Howell Book House, 1995.

About Health Care

American Kennel Club. *American Kennel Club Dog Care and Training.* New York: Howell Book House, 1991.

Carlson, Delbert, DVM, and James Giffen, MD. *Dog Owner's Home Veterinary Handbook.* New York: Howell Book House, 1992.

DeBitetto, James, DVM, and Sarah Hodgson. *You & Your Puppy.* New York: Howell Book House, 1995.

Schwartz, Stefanie, DVM. *First Aid for Dogs: An Owner's Guide to a Happy Healthy Pet.* New York: Howell Book House, 1998.

About Dog Shows

Hall, Lynn. *Dog Showing for Beginners.* New York: Howell Book House, 1994.

Vanacore, Connie. *Dog Showing, An Owner's Guide*. New York: Howell Book House, 1990.

About Training

Ammen, Amy. *Training in No Time*. New York: Howell Book House, 1995.

Dunbar, Ian, PhD, MRCVS. *Dr. Dunbar's Good Little Book*. James & Kenneth Publishers, 2140 Shattuck Ave. #2406, Berkeley, CA 94704. (510) 658-8588. Order from publisher.

Evans, Job Michael. *People, Pooches and Problems*. New York: Howell Book House, 1991.

About Activities

American Rescue Dog Association. *Search and Rescue Dogs*. New York: Howell Book House, 1991.

Davis, Kathy Diamond. *Therapy Dogs*. New York: Howell Book House, 1992.

O'Neil, Jackie. *All About Agility*. New York: Howell Book House, 1998.

Simmons-Moake, Jane. *Agility Training. The Fun Sport for All Dogs*. New York: Howell Book House, 1991.

MAGAZINES

The AKC GAZETTE, The Official Journal for the Sport of Purebred Dogs
American Kennel Club
51 Madison Ave.
New York, NY 10010

Dog Fancy
Fancy Publications
3 Burroughs
Irvine, CA 92718

Dog World
Maclean Hunter Publishing Corp.
29 N. Wacker Dr.
Chicago, IL 60606

True Grit
P.O. Box 4527
Lutherville, MD 21094-4527
The official publication of the Jack Russell Terrier Club of America.

MORE INFORMATION ON THE JACK RUSSSELL TERRIER

National Breed Club

THE JACK RUSSELL TERRIER CLUB OF AMERICA
P.O. Box 4527
Lutherville, MD 21094-4527
The club can provide you with information on all aspects of the breed, as well as the Russell Rescue contact nearest you. Inquire about membership.

RESOURCES

The American Kennel Club

The American Kennel Club, devoted to the advancement of purebred dogs, is the oldest and largest registry organization in this country. Every breed recognized by the AKC has a national (parent) club. National clubs are a great source of information on your breed. The affiliated clubs hold AKC events and use AKC rules to hold performance events, dog shows, educational programs, health clinics and training classes. The AKC staff is divided between offices in New York City and Raleigh, North Carolina. All registration functions are done in North Carolina.

For registration and performance events information, contact:

THE AMERICAN KENNEL CLUB
5580 Centerview Drive, Suite 200

Raleigh, NC 27606
Phone: (919)233-9767
Fax: (919)233-3627
E-mail: info@akc.org

For obedience information, contact:

THE AMERICAN KENNEL CLUB
51 Madison Ave.
New York, NY 10010
Phone: (212)696-8276
Fax: (212)696-8272
E-mail: www.akc.org

For information on AKC Companion Animal Recovery, contact:

Phone: (800)252-7894
Fax: (919)233-1290
E-mail: found@akc.org

REGISTRY ORGANIZATIONS

Registry organizations register purebred dogs.

CANADIAN KENNEL CLUB
100–89 Skyway Avenue
Etobicoke, Ontario
Canada M9W 6R4

UNITED KENNEL CLUB (UKC)
100 E. Kilgore Road
Kalamazoo, MI 49002

TRAINERS

ASSOCIATION OF PET DOG TRAINERS
P.O. Box 385
Davis, CA 95617
(800)PET-DOGS